Cambridge Elements

Elements in New Religious Movements
Series Editor
Rebecca Moore
San Diego State University
Founding Editor
†James R. Lewis
Wuhan University

MINORITY RELIGIONS, THE LAW, AND THE COURTS

Cases and Consequences

James T. Richardson
University of Nevada–Reno

Shaftesbury Road, Cambridge CB2 8EA, United Kingdom

One Liberty Plaza, 20th Floor, New York, NY 10006, USA

477 Williamstown Road, Port Melbourne, VIC 3207, Australia

314–321, 3rd Floor, Plot 3, Splendor Forum, Jasola District Centre,
New Delhi – 110025, India

103 Penang Road, #05–06/07, Visioncrest Commercial, Singapore 238467

Cambridge University Press is part of Cambridge University Press & Assessment,
a department of the University of Cambridge.

We share the University's mission to contribute to society through the pursuit of
education, learning and research at the highest international levels of excellence.

www.cambridge.org
Information on this title: www.cambridge.org/9781009617260

DOI: 10.1017/9781009617222

© James T. Richardson 2025

This publication is in copyright. Subject to statutory exception and to the
provisions of relevant collective licensing agreements, no reproduction of
any part may take place without the written permission of
Cambridge University Press & Assessment.

When citing this work, please include a reference to the
DOI 10.1017/9781009617222

First published 2025

A catalogue record for this publication is available from the British Library

ISBN 978-1-009-61723-9 Hardback
ISBN 978-1-009-61726-0 Paperback
ISSN 2635-232X (online)
ISSN 2635-2311 (print)

Cambridge University Press & Assessment has no responsibility for the persistence
or accuracy of URLs for external or third-party internet websites referred to in this
publication and does not guarantee that any content on such websites is, or will
remain, accurate or appropriate.

For EU product safety concerns, contact us at Calle de José Abascal, 56, 1°, 28003
Madrid, Spain, or email eugpsr@cambridge.org

Minority Religions, the Law, and the Courts

Cases and Consequences

Elements in New Religious Movements

DOI: 10.1017/9781009617222
First published online: November 2025

James T. Richardson
University of Nevada–Reno
Author for correspondence: James T. Richardson, jtr@unr.edu

Abstract: Using a socio-legal approach, this Element examines the complex intersections between minority religions, legal protections and restrictions, and the role played by courts in securing, or inhibiting, religious freedom. It considers the legal status of minority religious communities in selected countries from a comparative perspective, using theories from the sociology of law to explain how legal systems treat such religious groups. The role played by the European Court of Human Rights is also examined. A brief discussion considers how minority religions are dealt with in selected societies where authoritarian or theocratic systems of governance prevail. The Element then looks at how interactions between the law and the courts have led to changes, or "deformations," in selected well-known and controversial new and other minority religions. The Element concludes by observing how courts in Europe and North America have sometimes used cases involving minority faiths to promote their own agenda and authority, as well as to expand other important considerations, including religious freedom.

Keywords: Minority religions, new religious movements (NRMs), rule of law, rule by law, Supreme Court, European Court of Human Rights, sociology of law, autonomy of judicial systems, sociology of religious freedom, judicialization of religious freedom, deformation, community rights

© James T. Richardson 2025

ISBNs: 9781009617239 (HB), 9781009617260 (PB), 9781009617222 (OC)
ISSNs: 2635-232X (online), 2635-2311 (print)

Contents

Introduction. Historical, Structural, and Cultural Factors: A Socio-Legal Analysis   1

1 Theoretical Application to Specific Western Countries and Judicial Systems: United States, Germany, France, and Belgium   7

2 Theoretical Application to Specific Western Countries and Judicial Systems: Italy, the Netherlands, Denmark, and the United Kingdom   21

3 The European Court of Human Rights   26

4 Theoretical Application to Specific Non-Rule of Law Countries and Judicial Systems: China, Russia, and Iran   30

5 Law, the Courts, and "Deformation" of Minority Religions   35

6 Courts Using Minority Religions to Accomplish Their Own Agendas   50

Conclusions   55

References   59

Introduction. Historical, Structural, and Cultural Factors: A Socio-Legal Analysis

This Element reflects the findings of a long career that began with a keen interest in why many young and relatively affluent young people in the United States were joining new religious movements (NRMs) in the 1960s and 1970s. That interest led to considerable research on NRMs, some of which is reported herein. However, it quickly became obvious that many NRMs being studied were experiencing severe legal problems. Those difficulties led to requests from some groups for advice and legal assistance. These pleas for assistance persuaded me and other scholars that the legal attacks against them were based on pseudoscientific theories that did not comport with the findings of many sociologists and psychologists engaged in serious research on new religions (see Richardson 1985a, 1985c; Anthony 1990). This prompted me to obtain a law degree, acquired through five years of night school law classes. This led to my directing a graduate program for trial judges at the University of Nevada, Reno for thirty years. I taught seminars on uses of social and behavioral science evidence in courts and also directed dozens of theses and dissertations done by judges.[1] I also expanded my research efforts to many other countries and religious groups, focusing on the efforts to exert social control on new and minority religions both in the United States and abroad,[2] especially where judicial systems were involved.

I offer this autobiographical apologia so readers will know from the outset what my predispositions are, as well as my academic and legal background.[3]

---

[1] See Richardson, Robinson, and Schaar-Bias (2005) for a description of this large program, which is offered by the University of Nevada, Reno in conjunction with the National Judicial College and the National Council of Juvenile and Family Court Judges, both of which are affiliated with UNR. I have published a number of articles in law reviews and other academic journals dealing with use of such evidence in courts and other aspects of judicial systems in the United States and other countries. I have also held appointments at law schools and made presentations to judicial conferences in the United States and other countries.

[2] The term new and minority religions is meant to encompass the newer more exotic religious groups that developed within the United States in the 1960s and 1970s, some of which also spread to many other countries in the world. As researchers studied the diaspora of those groups in other countries, it became obvious that there were other small religious groups, including some that had developed in the nineteenth century in the United States, such as the Jehovah's Witnesses, which received the same critical treatment in other countries as did NRMs in the United States. Hence, other scholars and I began using the terms "minority religion" and "new and minority religions" to encompass all smaller religious groups that encountered difficulties as they attempted to remain viable and promote their beliefs and practices within the societies in which they existed.

[3] Appreciation is expressed to scholars who assisted in coverage of the specific countries and religious groups discussed in this Element, as well as the representatives of some of the NRMs and other minority faiths included. Special thanks to Rebecca Moore, the editor

The Element itself provides evidence that has led me to these views.[4] That evidence will be organized in three separate but interwoven discussions that offer a socio-legal interpretation of the interaction of law and religion in contemporary societies. The Element first looks at how new and older minority faiths are dealt with in legal/judicial systems in selected countries and in the European context with the ECtHR. Second, it looks at how these encounters with the legal systems have changed those religious groups in sometimes dramatic ways. Finally, it addresses how courts have accepted and used cases involving new and other minority religions to expand their own geographic purview and authority.

Historical, Structural, and Cultural Factors: A Socio-Legal Analysis

All religious groups operate within the confines of the legal structure of the societies in which they reside (Beckford and Richardson 2007; Richardson 2016). Doing so for favored groups, which might be the de facto or de jure official religion of a society, is usually quite different from the experience of newer and minority faiths. Indeed, these dominant faiths may take for granted many privileges and advantages in part because they have been able to influence the development of a legal structure that protects the privileged status they enjoy. Moreover, those in positions of power in society may share the values and beliefs of the dominant faith, allowing a degree of cultural intimacy that facilitates and protects the functioning of the dominant group.[5] The situation for minority faiths is, however, quite different. Often the beliefs and practices of such smaller groups are at odds with the values of the dominant culture, thus calling attention to the group and perhaps leading to levels of animus and efforts to exert social control. Such control efforts can vary greatly in intensity, ranging from various forms of harassment being allowed, or even officially encouraged, to direct official governmental efforts to suppress a minority religion (Richardson 2016). Such efforts at social control of minority religions may lead to new legislation and often involve actions

---

of this series, who is a superb editor and writer. Her considerable efforts made this a much more cogent and readable contribution.

[4] For more details on this personal journey, see Richardson (1991). For discussion of significant involvement in some major legal actions involving NRMs, see Richardson (1996), and especially Richardson, "The Accidental Expert" (1998a).

[5] See Donald Black's (1976, 1998) discussions of how legal structures are established to serve the interests of the more powerful in society, as well as his concept of cultural distance or intimacy and its effects on human behavior. See Richardson (2004, 11–15; 2016) for discussion of Black's overall theoretical approach as applicable to NRMs.

within judicial systems (Richardson 1995a, 2015c, 2021b). This Element therefore analyzes such efforts, which obviously affect minority religions as they attempt to survive in sometimes hostile environments and promote their ideas and practices. These control mechanisms also offer opportunities for judicial systems to expand their own purview and authority.

Even within the broad category of nations that purport to operate within the rule of law[6] and promote democracy (Fox 2020), differences exist. Implementation of the rule of law varies considerably within the Western nations and is virtually nonexistent in more authoritarian societies. Rule of law nations usually make efforts through their constitutions and legislation to maintain significant separation of religion and government, with the United States cited frequently as an example.[7] This model can allow and encourage a more competitive situation that facilitates some cultural and social space for minority religions to develop and function (Stark and Finke 1992; McGraw 2003). Some rule of law societies have granted significant rights and privileges to a particular religion, or religions, either through constitutional provisions, by law, or historical precedent. Such societies adhere to the rule of law, but with specific important historical precedents. In such situations the dominant religious tradition may attempt to guard its rights and privileges against challenges from possible competitors by seeking alliances with dominant institutional and political entities in order to influence legislation and its implementation (Fox 2020). Such dominant faiths may even enjoy explicit protections in founding documents or have special concords established by law or treaty. How such protections are developed is, according to William Chambliss (1993), a dialectical agency-oriented process that reveals the values of those in power positions within a society. Some of those protections may result in quite explicit efforts at control, or even eradication, of minority religious groups.

Within nations that adhere to the rule of law, there are many differences historically and culturally that must be examined for full understanding of

---

[6] Rule of law nations typically operate with shared governance between executive, legislative, and judicial branches, with the judicial system having authority to challenge and overrule actions of the legislative and executive branches if actions taken by those entities do not comport with the governing documents (such as a constitution) of the society. See Tamanaha (2004) for more detail on this important concept that is often used to describe Western-oriented democracies.

[7] Some controversy has developed recently concerning separation of church and state in America with the US Congress and the Supreme Court vying for preeminence in this area in a manner that seems to privilege certain forms of religion – actions that would seem violative of the anti-establishment clause of the Constitution (see Hamilton 2003; Richardson and McGraw 2019; and Liptak 2025).

the legal status of minority religions. A theoretical analysis of the "sociology of religious freedom" (Richardson 2006b, 2007) examines important specifics, including the degree of *religious diversity* in societies. This diversity has occurred because of the considerable movement of people facilitated by modern means of travel, and because wars and other disruptive circumstances in their host societies have forced them to flee to safety. Religious diversity can force governments to attempt to manage religion to limit potential conflict and even violence between groups. Sometimes governments may decide to allow a degree of legal pluralism in a society, which grants some autonomy to specific religious groups to function in defined areas of life according to their own norms and rules.[8] Domestic relations (divorce, child custody, inheritance, and so on) is an area where some Western societies have granted, by either law or tradition, a degree of autonomy to Jewish and Muslim groups to manage such issues (Berger 2013; Witte and Nichols 2013; Broyde 2017; Benhalim 2019a, 2019b).[9] Some Western nations have granted limited autonomy to indigenous peoples, which is another example of legal pluralism.

There are other important considerations as well if one is to grasp the level of religious freedom granted minority religions (Richardson 2006b).[10] The key characteristics of legal systems include pervasiveness, centralization, degree of autonomy, and whether a legal system operates in an adversarial or inquisitorial manner. *Pervasiveness* refers to how much legal considerations penetrate the everyday life of citizens in society. In some societies many if not most aspects of the lives of citizens are affected by laws and law-like considerations promulgated by governmental bureaucracies. The growing tendency for governments in some contemporary societies to surveil their citizens is an extreme example of pervasiveness. It occurs in the United States (Richardson and Robbins 2010), but even more pervasively in some authoritarian societies such as China (Edelman and Richardson 2003, 2005) and Iran (Adeliyan Tous and Richardson 2024). However, there are many other ways that governments touch the

---

[8] See Tamanaha (2008), Richardson (2011b), and Possamai, Richardson, and Turner (2024) for discussions of legal pluralism; see Richardson and Springer (2013) for a theoretical discussion of legal pluralism and Islam; and Richardson (2015a) for an application of William Chambliss' theoretical approach to the development of Shari'a in some Western societies.

[9] Granting a degree of legal pluralism for Muslim and Jewish groups in Muslim minority countries is often quite contentious as shown in Richardson and Turner (2024) and Turner and Richardson (2024).

[10] For a somewhat different but quite useful analysis of the conditions for religious freedom, see Fox (2021), who uses a large international data set to demonstrate that religious freedom has limitations in most nations in the world, including even the most liberal ones.

lives of citizens in today's world, some of which attempt to manage the religious life of citizens for, among other possible reasons, the management of potential conflict in an increasingly pluralistic world.

Centralization refers to whether government power and control is consolidated in one location and bureaucratic structure, or instead its functions are shared with other locations and bureaucratic structures in a more federalized system. The United States is an example of some sharing of power, with many functions left to the states by virtue of the Tenth Amendment to the Constitution.[11] Germany also operates a somewhat federalized system, with considerable power granted to the 16 *Länder* (states) making up the country. Many other nations, both Western and non-Western, are much more centralized, thus potentially offering more control over all aspects of life for their citizens, including in their religion. Thus, the highly centralized government in France has launched major efforts to limit, control, or even dissolve some minority religions (see, e.g., Richardson 2004; Wright and Palmer 2016; Adeliyan Tous, Richardson, and Taghipour 2023; Westbrook 2024).

Autonomy of the judiciary is quite important to consider when examining factors influencing religious freedom in a society, even in countries where the other branches of government have been quite critical of new and minority religious groups (Richardson 2006b; Finke and Mataic 2021). Societies vary greatly in the levels of independence granted to judicial systems. Some such as Germany, Italy, the United Kingdom, Canada, Australia, the United States, and even France and Belgium have judicial systems with considerable independence from other institutional structures. These courts have the inherent power to overrule actions of the legislative and executive branches in some circumstances, and their judicial systems are not usually dominated by any political party, the military, or a dominant church.[12] These societies have constitutions, laws, and historical

---

[11] The Tenth Amendment states, "The powers not delegated to the United States by the Constitution, nor prohibited by it to the States, are reserved to the States, respectively, or to the people." Given the significant cultural differences among and between different regions of the United States, the accruing of power to the States – the "states' rights" movement – could be thought of as a special form of legal pluralism. There was a clear demonstration of the relative autonomy of individual states in the religion area when, after the Religious Freedom Restoration Act was deemed not applicable to state and local governments by a decision of the United States Supreme Court, over two dozen states passed "mini-RFAs" to protect religious freedom (Richardson 1999a).

[12] Richardson (2006a) lauded the independence and power of the Hungarian Constitutional Court, because in the 1990s it had in fact been a rare case of a society formerly dominated by the Soviet Union that had developed into a "rule of law" society with a very strong judicial system. Kim Scheppele (2003) referred to this powerful court as a "courtocracy."

precedents that offer protections for human and civil rights, including religious freedom. Thus, if individuals holding positions of power within judicial systems share values that include religious freedom, then those values should be manifest in decisions made concerning religion and minority religious groups (Richardson and Van Driel 1994; Richardson 2004). Such a situation has been described as demonstrating the "judicialization of religious freedom."[13] Of course, minority religious do not always prevail in the legal arena, but they can at least be heard in countries operating under the rule of law and sometimes do prevail for understandable reasons.[14]

Another characteristic worth noting concerns whether a society has a functioning system of lawyers willing and able to represent religious groups that are involved in legal actions. The adversarial system that operates in the United States is an example of such a system that allows lawyers who are so inclined to act as advocates defending religious freedom (Richardson 2021c). Western societies such as France which operate the judicial system in an inquisitorial fashion are less prone to hear strong defenses of religious freedom in cases involving minority religions. In such systems, minority religions are disadvantaged unless the judge or representative of a governmental agency dealing with religion cases values religious freedom and has the autonomy to exercise their values.

The context of rule of law contrasts sharply with societies such as China, Russia, and Iran where minority religious groups may be defined as enemies of the State and thus are not allowed to defend themselves in any forum. These and other nations use the judicial system to promote the interests of the regime, a situation sometimes referred to as "rule by law." Rule by law describes a system of governance in which the government

---

However, that situation changed dramatically shortly thereafter, and Hungary is now considered an authoritarian state with all governmental entities, including the courts, subservient to the State. See Bánkuti, Halmai, and Scheppele (2013).

[13] The judicialization of religious freedom refers a situation where issues concerning religious freedom are referred (or left) to the courts to resolve and the courts adopt a posture toward such claims that is protective of such claims. This can occur only in societies that have a relatively autonomous judicial system. See Richardson (2015c, 2021b) for details and examples.

[14] See Richardson (2021c) for analysis of reasons why minority religions sometimes prevail in legal actions; see also Richardson and Bellanger (2014), and Barker and Richardson (2021) for examples of such situations. Of particular note is the role that "third-party partisans" – a concept from Donald Black's work (see Black and Baumgartner 1999) – play in securing positive results from court involvement of minority religions. Examples of third-party partisans include lawyers available to represent minority religions in court actions in adversarial systems, involvement of NGOs and "cause lawyers" promoting religious freedom, academic scholars getting involved as consultants and expert witnesses, and even the courts themselves when doing so will help promote a court's agenda (see Richardson 2017b, 2021b on this latter point).

can create and enforce laws as it sees fit, without regard for the impact on people's freedoms or interests. This type of political system has one all-powerful entity, the executive branch – which might be dominated by a political party, the military, a dominant church, or a combination of such entities – able to enact any law it desires, usually through actions of a compliant legislative branch, with law enforcement and ultimately the courts enforcing those edicts through actions and rulings based on the law.

The various historical and structural factors delineated above obviously underpin efforts to exert control over both new and older minority religions in increasingly religiously diverse contemporary societies. Social control of such groups is obviously made easier in more pervasive and centralized systems of governance, especially if there are no competing institutions such as a functioning sector of entities, such as NGOs, that make up civil society, or an autonomous judicial system with the power to limit such efforts. In such societies the effects on religious groups of efforts at control are more effective, as the groups, in order to survive, make efforts to accommodate to the desires of entities within society that wield power. The degree of judicial autonomy plays a major role as well, whether demonstrated by rulings that offer some protections to minority religious groups or by efforts of the courts to extend and expand their own purview and authority.

This Element emphasizes that rule of law nations, although sometimes quite varied in historical factors and culture noted above, offer more opportunities to protect religious freedom. The typical tripartite political arrangements in such nations, as well as their underlying governing documents, usually afford protections for civil and human rights, including freedom of religion. In sharp contrast, rule by law nations with one dominant political organization do not brook any competition and religious groups are often viewed as a challenge to the authority of the state. Political authorities in such societies assume that any religious organization that gains a following must be controlled or abolished, regardless of what might be contained in constitutions and other governing documents. And in such societies the law becomes a tool with which to exert control, placing all religions, not only new and minority religions, at risk.

1 Theoretical Application to Specific Western Countries and Judicial Systems: United States, Germany, France, and Belgium

There is tremendous variety in how religion and religious minorities are dealt with by governments among rule of law countries. The next two sections apply theories of law to specific Western countries. Section 1 focuses on nations with mixed records on religious freedom, while Section 2 concentrates on countries demonstrating more opportunities for tolerance and freedom for minority religions. Each contains brief descriptions country-by-country that highlight similarities and differences in the approach to religious minorities.

This section examines the United States, Germany, France, and Belgium, four nations that differ in their history and culture, as well as their treatment of minority faiths. The United States serves as the initial focus for several reasons. For one thing, many of the newer religious groups that have since spread to European nations and beyond developed initially within the United States in the 1960s and 1970s. Some of the more controversial older minority faiths, such as the Jehovah's Witnesses, developed in the United States before also expanding into Europe and other countries. Also, the United States has been the major location where freedom of religion as a workable concept was developed in its early history, and this concept has played a major role in defining American society since that time. Germany and France were selected for more detailed treatment because they are dominant societies within the European context, with both taking a much more openly critical stance of minority religious groups and their assumed effects on society. Germany has taken a somewhat measured stance concerning minority faiths but has made warning about the alleged dangers of participation in such groups a theme of its governmental bureaucracy in the twenty-first century. France, particularly, has become something of an outlier among Western nations in the animus displayed toward any non-Catholic religion expressions. Belgium is included because it closely follows the French approach to minority faiths.

United States

The United States has served as a model rule of law state since its inception nearly two and a half centuries ago. The establishment of a strong tripartite system of government with its inherent checks and balances has served as an example for many other nations since the Republic was established. Recently and regrettably, the status of the United States as a rule of law nation is being called into question since the election of President Trump to a second term. He has issued dozens of edicts that seem to circumvent statutes and constitutional provisions and seems intent on ignoring the statutory roles of Congress and the Judiciary. His administration has refused to obey selected court orders when some of his directives have been challenged. Moreover, some in his administration have stated that as president he can ignore court rulings and have argued that judges who rule against him should be impeached. Erwin Chemerinsky, Dean of the Law School at University of California, Berkeley, among many others, has offered an analysis of the current situation in the United States (Chemerinsky 2025). For an international perspective on what is happening in the United States, see the discussion by Hans Petter Graver, former Dean of the University of Oslo Law School (Graver 2025a). He compares what is happening in the United States to what occurred in Germany in the 1930s, as well as in some contemporary Eastern European nations (Graver 2025a).[15]

Thus, it is unclear at the time of this writing whether the United States will persist as a rule of law nation. Nonetheless, historically America has a vibrant history of allowing, and even indirectly promoting, the growth of minority religions because of the First Amendment of the Constitution, which protects the free exercise of religion and has historically disallowed the establishment of a state religion. In addition, the country is a federated system with considerable power left to the individual states, thus its federal government has been less centralized and pervasive than most European countries. As a result, and with the tradition of "separation of church and state" at the national level, the country is replete with various religious experiments, some of which have developed into large international religions, such as the Church of Jesus Christ of Latter-day Saints (Mormons), and the Jehovah's Witnesses. Other examples of American-born religious groups of note include the Church of Christ, Scientist (aka Christian Science), and the Seventh-day Adventists.

In the second half of the twentieth century, America also saw the origination or growth of a number of NRMs that gained impetus to become international movements. Examples include the Church of Scientology, the Unification Church (now the Family Federation for World Peace and Unification), the International Society for Krishna Consciousness (known familiarly as the Hare Krishnas), and the Children of God (COG) (now The Family International, TFI). Some smaller new religious groups using controlled substances or sacrificing various animals as part of their rituals have emerged in the twenty-first century in North America or were imported from abroad (see Ward 2009; Richardson and Shoemaker 2014; Stoddard 2024). Although these newer religious

---

[15] Graver (2025b) has also written forcefully about the need for judges to resist intimidation and their responsibility to help maintain the rule of law.

groups often encountered serious difficulties, including legal actions against them, they could rely to some extent on protections offered by the US Constitution when required to defend themselves in court or to bring actions to defend their interests.[16] The adversarial system extant in the US legal system also offered opportunities to have strong advocacy at their disposal in such actions. This was occasionally accomplished by the development of in-house legal prowess (e.g., Jehovah's Witnesses and Scientology), but often it involved securing support from legal or academic experts or NGOs interested in religious freedom. Some NRMs and older minority religions (see Richardson 2015b) won many cases in the US Supreme Court or from governmental agencies such as the Internal Revenue System (e.g., Richardson 2009; Roux 2021). Although the experience for minority religions with courts was sometimes positive, courts also found new interpretations of applicable legal provisions that limited or even cancelled those victories (Richardson 1995a, 1998b).[17]

In the twenty-first century there has been a major shift in the way minority religions are treated in the United States as a result of a significant Supreme Court decision in 1990 (*Smith* v. *Oregon*), which took away some long-standing protections for minority religious groups. The case involved two drug counselors in Oregon who were members of the Native American Church, which used peyote as part of its sacred rituals. Their employment was terminated, and they sued, claiming this violated their religious freedom. They won at the trial level and with the Oregon Supreme Court but eventually lost on appeal by the State of Oregon with a Supreme Court ruling that dramatically changed how such matters were to be viewed. The new guiding principle became that if a law is facially neutral, then it is valid even if it infringed on the religious freedom of some individuals and groups.[18]

---

[16] The protections offered by the US Constitution also had the paradoxical effect of giving rise to self-help measures, such as deprogramming, which gained considerable momentum in the United States and then spread to some other countries, notably Japan (Shupe, Spielmann, and Stigal 1977; Bromley and Richardson 1983; LeMoult 1983; Richardson 2011a). Those protections also encouraged the use of the courts instead of other governmental entities, as has been the case in Germany and France, to exert control over minority religions.

[17] In the 1970s and 1980s, the Hare Krishna practice of soliciting funds in airports and at large gatherings and the Unification Church practice of street solicitation for funds eventually found their options limited by court rulings allowing time and place restrictions justified on public safety concerns (Richardson 1998b; Rochford 1988).

[18] https://constitutioncenter.org/the-constitution/supreme-court-case-library/employment-division-v-smith#:~:text=In%201990%2C%20the%20Supreme%20Court,peyote%20during%20a%20religious%20ceremony.

This decision was viewed by many as a contraction of longstanding religious freedom rights. The situation led to a dramatic Congressional reaction with the near-unanimous passage of the Religious Freedom Restoration Act (RFRA) in 1996. The Religious Land Use and Institutional Persons Act (RLUIPA) in 2000 affirmed and even extended traditional protections for various religious activities.[19] These two acts offered grounds to defend religious freedom for minority religions, including even for prisoners and members of the military (see McGraw and Richardson, 2020). Some resistance to these broader options has developed, however, as a conflict between some religious freedom claims and rights of some legally protected minorities, such as LGBQT persons, has developed in recent case law (Richardson and McGraw 2019).[20]

Germany

Germany's religious history is quite different from that of the United States in that the region has been the location of devastating religious wars in its past.[21] In modern times, however, Germany has managed to develop a society based on a dual Catholic-Protestant arrangement that has been relatively peaceful. Indeed, as James Beckford (1985, 251) notes in his discussion of why and how this peaceful coexistence developed, the cooperative religious landscape is sometimes credited with contributing to the relative peace and prosperity of Germany in the post-WWII environment.[22] This overall situation of seeming agreement on how German society should function in the postwar environment has not, however,

---

[19] RLUIPA was passed after the Supreme Court ruled that RFRA was not applicable to state and local governments. RLUIPA extended protections much more broadly than had been the case, however, as it exerted federal authority over land use decisions (zoning) and over treatment of prisoners and other incarcerated individuals, both of which areas had been left to the states to regulate heretofore.

[20] See Marci Hamilton (2003, 2005) for vigorous critiques of RFRA and RLUIPA. Hamilton is the attorney who argued the case before the Supreme Court that resulted in RFRA not being applied to state and local governments. Also see Liptak (2025) for a recent assessment of how religions are winning in the US Supreme Court, at the expense of some other rights as cases are being decided in ways that reveal a new emphasis on the establishment clause.

[21] Derek Davis (2000) offers a succinct history of these religious conflicts in Germany's history even as he laments growing anti-minority religion bias in contemporary Germany. See Zoehrer (2021) and Roux (2021) for specific examples of legal efforts to impede activities of two NRMs there, the Unification Church and Scientology.

[22] Note that the welcoming of large numbers of Muslims into Germany after World War II to help rebuild the society led to challenges as Germany has tried to find ways to integrate what turned out to be long-term residents of culturally different peoples into the society. Currently Muslims, largely from Turkey, account for about 7 percent of Germany's population. See Aries, Sahinöz, and Richardson (2023) for discussion of this situation.

precluded considerable concern about the rise of interest among a small minority of youth in some of the NRMs that have come to Germany, many of which are defined as American products. Consequently, there have been a number of official efforts to understand and control participation in what are referred to in Germany as "youth religions" or "youth sects." Given the small size and numbers of these groups in Germany, it seems that the focus on them has all the trappings of a moral panic (Cohen 1972; Richardson and Introvigne 2007), illustrating Beckford's point that the reaction to newer religions is of more interest than the religious groups themselves (1985, 11).

In the United States, battles over NRMs often were fought within the judicial system because of First Amendment protections afforded religion; in addition, the nation had a history of church-state separation. In Germany the situation is considerably different, with there being a much closer relationship between the dual religious hierarchy and the government. There is a view that the government in Germany is more paternalistic toward its citizens than the US government (Beckford 1985). Indeed, there has been a working relationship between certain governmental entities, such as the Federal Ministry for Youth, Family, and Health, and the national hierarchies of the Catholic and Protestant churches, both of which have devoted considerable resources to the perceived problem of the new youth religions. The ministry, which has a constitutional edict to protect German citizens, has used this as a justification to produce widely circulated publications warning of the threat of youth religions, and these have been used as materials in schools throughout Germany. These publications have also been promoted by mass media outlets in Germany that have contributed to concern among the general population, thereby contributing to the moral panic. The ministry has sponsored special programs and financed research projects directed at promoting the official view of the new religions (Beckford 1985, 257–9). The ministry has also cooperated with various anticult organizations that have been developed in Germany, and it has taken the lead in having other federal ministries join in efforts to control the supposed menace of youth religions.[23]

The debate in Germany over youth religions, especially Scientology, led directly to the establishment in 1996 by the German Bundestag

---

[23] In some parts of Germany, a "sect filter" has been implemented requiring citizens who seek public employment or benefits from the state to swear that they are not members of Scientology or other "sekten." See https://bitterwinter.org/sect-filters-in-germany-institutionalizing-the-anti-cult-narrative/.

of an Enquete Commission on "So-called Sects and Psychogroups." The Commission took its remit seriously and had 49 sessions over two years. It also requested that scholars in the area of study conduct research for the Commission before issuing its report (Seiwert 2004). The final report in 1998 was, however, quite controversial. Hubert Seiwert, a scholar of some repute who was appointed to the Commission as an expert on religious groups, even drafted a critical minority report that was attached to the final official report and signed by two other Commission members.[24] Seiwert noted that no accusations of criminal or unlawful activities by any of the religious groups could be substantiated – except possibly for Scientology, but even that was not certain. However, the Commission, which included some well-known anticult-oriented members, maintained a negative posture toward the groups that had given rise to the establishment of the Commission when it made recommendations. Seiwert notes that the report had little impact on governmental policies with the exception of one major change that allowed the government to ban associations, including new religious groups, under certain conditions (Seiwert, 2004, 98).[25]

Although most issues concerning religious minorities were not dealt with by the German judicial system, one episode deserves mention. The legal status of "public corporation" in the German Constitution, with its many attendant rights and privileges, had been granted to the two major religious organizations, Catholic and Protestant, along with several other minority faiths. However, it was denied to the Jehovah's Witnesses in 1993 in the *Bundesland* of Berlin for reasons that were not authorized in governing documents, a clear demonstration of the role of public animus toward the group.[26] The Witnesses sued and won at the trial court level but lost on appeal to the Berlin Administrative Court. After years of legal battles back and forth between various courts, the well-respected Constitutional Court of Germany finally ruled definitively in favor of the Witnesses in 2000, a major victory for the Witnesses in the *Bundesland* (state) of Berlin. However, although this decision was an important precedent, public corporation status was not automatically granted in the other 14 *Länder*

---

[24] Seiwert (2004) discusses the acrimony that was often a part of confidential meetings of the Commission – confrontations that even included an early effort to have him removed from the body with false accusations that he was himself a Scientologist.

[25] Although some religious groups, especially Scientology, fought against this change in the law, so far it has only been used against Islamic groups defined as terrorist groups. Indeed, the new law may have been motivated mainly by anti-Islam sentiments in Germany (Seiwert 2004, 99).

[26] Refusal to take part in public elections was cited (Seiwert 2004, 99).

in Germany, leading to more legal battles.[27] Finally, in 2015 public corporation status for the Witnesses was gained the last *Länder*. These cases brought by the Witnesses demonstrated the value of having an autonomous judicial system (even though the final resolution took a while) if religious freedom is to be protected.

Germany, by virtue of its membership in the Council of Europe (CoE) and being a signatory to the European Convention on Human Rights (ECHR) is, of course, subject to the jurisdiction of the European Court of Human Rights (ECtHR). One ECtHR decision in 2008 concerning Germany's right (or responsibility) to warn citizens of potential harm is worth noting. The *Leela Förderkreis E.V. and Others v. Germany* case was brought by three Osho organizations because of their dissatisfaction with a German Constitutional Court decision on language used to describe the groups in official government publications. That decision, while disallowing some negative terms used – including destructive, pseudo-religious, and manipulative – had allowed continued use of other terms the groups found offensive – cult, NRM, and psychogroup. The groups submitted the matter to the ECtHR that ruled that those terms did not violate Article 9 (freedom of religion and belief) of the European Convention, thus granting considerable deference to the State as it made efforts to inform citizens of perceived danger.[28]

France

France has a much more centralized national governance structure and also has a unique religious history.[29] The anti-religion sentiments that exploded in the French Revolution led to establishment of an official policy of *laïcité* adopted in 1905. The constitutional principal of secularism

---

[27] See Besier and Besier (2000) for discussion of the long legal battle over the status of the Witnesses in Germany and see Besier (2018) and Seiwert (2015) for discussions of how the battles over recognition continued within the 15 Länders that make up Germany.

[28] The ECtHR did find a violation of Article 6 (right to a fair trial) because of the long time the case was pending in German courts. As will be shown in Section 3, the ECtHR has in the twenty-first century shown much more deference to member states (particularly most original members of the CoE) and allowed historical and cultural values to dominate and overcome some claims of religious discrimination (Beaman 2012–2013, 2024; Richardson 2019; Breskaya, Giordan, and Richardson 2024).

[29] This discussion summarizes the findings of Adeliyan Tous, Richardson, and Taghipour (2023), who present a detailed discussion of how the law has been used in France in efforts to manage and control minority religions over several decades. The authors demonstrate how law can be used to *limit* religious freedom. This original analysis applies theories from the sociology of law to developments in France, but that discussion will not be included herein.

in France, *laïcité*, has deterred the presence of any forms or symbols of religion in public forums and discourse. This policy – developed with Catholicism, traditional Protestantism, and Judaism as the major cultural presences – seemed adequate as a way to manage and control religion in order not to disrupt society. However, the policy has encountered considerable difficulty in the late twentieth and early twenty-first centuries with the influx into France of millions of Muslims from North Africa. Muslims now constitute about 10 percent of the French population. The presence of a number of older minority religions – Mormons, Jehovah's Witnesses, and others – along with the development in France of newer ones that espouse views about their dress and activities that are contrary to the tenets of *laïcité* has put strains on that policy.[30] The situation in France has become fraught with difficulties. Moreover, responses that the French government has made have resulted in it becoming an outlier in Western Europe in how religion is managed (see Palmer 2008; Ollion 2013). It has passed laws against Muslim women's head garb being worn in public and when working in public jobs, such as teaching or even in private employment (Adrian 2016; Vickers 2021; Richardson 2022). Its governmental institutions have been encouraged to pursue punitive measures against various minority faiths, efforts that often have involved state-financed anticult organizations.

Efforts by various entities within the French establishment, including government, religious groups, and mass media, were undergirded by the French version of secularism, referred to by some as "assertive secularism" (Kuru 2009). However, it is clear that some of the dramatic actions taken were given impetus by a series of tragic events involving some of the newer religious groups. Some French parents were already expressing concern about their children showing interest in the new and esoteric groups. Events such as the Jonestown mass murders and suicides in 1978 (Hall 1987; Moore 2022), and the burning of the Waco, Texas compound in 1993 with eighty Branch Davidians and four law enforcement officers dying in the 51-day siege (Wright 1995) were extremely disturbing. Most influential in France, however, were the Solar Temple murders and suicides that occurred in Switzerland, Quebec, and France between 1994 and 1997. The deaths of 74 individuals (Mayer 1996; Bogdan 2011) exacerbated fears and set off a major moral panic in

---

[30] See Beckford 2004a; Altglas 2010; Bacquet 2012; Dericquebourg 2017; and S. Davis 2020 for background on *laïcité* and current issues involved in managing nontraditional faiths in France.

the nation (Richardson and Introvigne 2007). The moral panic greatly facilitated the dramatic actions taken in France in the twenty-first century to control or even eradicate minority religious groups.

Even before then, concern over minority religions came to the fore in the 1980s, leading to the first Parliamentary action – the development of a report on the issue (Adeliyan Tous, Richardson, and Taghipour 2023; Westbrook 2024). No formal action was taken at that time, however, and it was not until the mid-1990s that serious efforts were made by the government to address the perceived peril from groups defined as threatening the French way of life by attracting French young people. A "parliamentary commission of inquiry on sects in France" was established which, after only twenty-one hours of confidential hearings with individuals and organizations (including the Catholic Church) critical of the new groups, issued its now-infamous list of over 170 groups that should be controlled or even forced out of France due to their use of "mental manipulation" to recruit young people (Anthony and Robbins 2004; Duvert 2004). Being included on the list has had quite extreme consequences for some of the groups: some are unable to build or rent facilities for meetings and many experience harassment by governmental entities and private parties. Some individuals have lost (or been unable to find) jobs if it became known they were members of some of the forbidden groups (Palmer 2011).

The Parliamentary Commission then issued an additional lengthy report cataloging what it defined as problematic groups, discussed how they were organized in simplistic and inaccurate terms, and listed many problems supposedly caused by them. Although acknowledging that the legal structure in France should be adequate to deal with the problem of *sectes*, the report nonetheless proposed a number of additional governmental actions that should be taken to control them (Adeliyan Tous et al. 2023, 8–11). This recommendation led to the establishment by then French President Jacques Chirac of a special "Interministerial Observatory on Cults" reporting directly to the prime minister, who was charged with coordinating activities to control *sectes*.

In 1998 the Observatory issued a report calling for radical changes in the law to facilitate its efforts, including granting private anticult groups the right to bring legal actions against the groups, a very radical proposal that was approved by the Parliament.[31] In addition, various governmental entities set up training programs for police, state prosecutors, judges, and

---

[31] Some of these private groups were already being partially supported with government funding. See Dericquebourg 2017; Duval 2017; and Human Rights Without Frontiers 2025.

teachers to make them aware of the alleged dangers the *sectes* posed for French society (Palmer 2011, 17).

Even those proposals and activities were unsatisfactory for some political leaders, leading to a second effort that included establishing a Commission of Inquiry into the Financial, Asset and Tax Situation of Sects, as well as Their Economic Activities and Their Relations with Economic and Financial Circles, established on December 15, 1998, and headed by Parliamentary Deputies Jacques Guyard and Jean-Pierre Brard. This new commission focused on the finances of the *sectes* and how they raised and managed funds. These efforts led to new and intrusive reporting requirements on group finances, with huge taxes being levied against some of the groups. These actions eventually resulted in the ECtHR ruling against France for its actions, in an unprecedented decision.[32] The new commission also had proposed creating a new crime of "mental manipulation," a proposal that was eventually abandoned; nevertheless, the crime of mental manipulation circuitously found its way into current statutes, using the substitute language "the fraudulent abuse of the state of ignorance or weakness," but with the identical description used to define mental manipulation (see Adeliyan Tous, et al. 2023). Eventually a new statute, referred to as the About-Picard law, was passed on May 30, 2001, containing many new measures that would supposedly facilitate controlling *sectes* (Duvert 2004). That law, however, has *not* been aggressively implemented against some of the more controversial groups, such as Scientology and Jehovah's Witnesses, and has instead been more broadly used against New Age types of movements and other organizations (Altglas 2010; Palmer 2022).[33]

The moral panic in France continued and there were other efforts to take additional actions against minority religions. In 2006 yet another commission was established focusing on allegations of child abuse in *sectes*.[34] After another biased study process, the Commission issued a 789-page report with fifty specific recommendations. However, the report did not lead directly to any further legislation at that time.

The concern within the ranks of some governmental entities in France was also on display in the 2020s, with proposed legislation rewriting some

---

[32] See discussion of this important case in Lykes and Richardson (2014, 180–2), which was the first Article 9 case lost by France in the ECtHR.

[33] This lack of action against Scientology and the Witnesses may have been motivated by the belief that if such a course of action was taken, both groups would carry the cases to the ECtHR, allowing judicial scrutiny over the policies developed by France.

[34] See Richardson (1999b) for discussion of the anticult movements shift from brainwashing claims to those involving child abuse.

criminal statutes to attempt to deal with Islamic radicalism. However, the language of the proposal, which was couched in terms of opposing *separatisme* (separatism), would also encompass *sectes*, and potentially other types of groups. The proposal was subsequently approved and thus became another law that could be used against minority faiths.

In 2024 yet another, more serious effort to control *sectes* was made. The new proposition was referred to as a "law reinforcing the fight against cultic deviance." This proposal, which offered some major amendments to the About-Picard law,[35] was rejected by the Senate. However, the Assembly passed the proposal, and under French Parliamentary rules it became law. A request was later made by more than sixty senators that the Constitutional Council of France review the new law to see if its provisions complied with the French Constitution (Introvigne 2024a). The Council did review the new statute, limiting its application somewhat, but it allowed most provisions to be enforced.[36]

The new statute was strongly supported by elements of the French governmental structure, which suggests that Altglas's claim that there might be a movement within the government to limit anti-*secte* efforts may not represent the current state of affairs in France (Altglas 2010). It remains to be seen what the future will hold for minority faiths in France. Meanwhile, the long list of forbidden groups still exists, thus limiting the religious expression for many in French society, although some French courts and the ECtHR have occasionally issued rulings limiting governmental actions against minority faiths.

Belgium

The Belgian political approach to minority faiths has been considerably influenced by France as it has adopted a critical approach to newer groups that have come to Belgium in the twenty-first century, as well to groups that have existed in Belgium for decades.[37] The long history of how Belgium

---

[35] Two major changes included provisions that created a new crime of "psychological subjection," that is making efforts to solicit someone to join a group a crime per se, regardless of the situation or the effects on the individual. Also included were provisions to make it a crime to attempt to dissuade anyone from accepting medical provisions or vaccinations generally approved by the medical community, a provision that appeared to be aimed at the anti-vaccination movement that developed during the Covid pandemic, as well as the refusal of blood transfusions by the Jehovah's Witnesses (Introvigne 2024a).

[36] For details on this decision see www.conseil-constitutionnel.fr/actualites/communique/decision-n-2024-865-dc-du-7-mai-2024-communique-de-presse.

[37] Special appreciation is expressed to Willy Fautré and Massimo Introvigne for assistance in preparing this discussion on Belgium, as well as other areas included in the effort.

manages religious organizations is presented in Fautré (2021), who notes that particularly the Flemish parts of Belgium follow the French approach to minority faiths, attempting to control them and to warn citizens about their alleged dangers. In 1998, the government established the Center for Information and Advice on Harmful Cultic Organizations, following similar efforts in France.[38] In June of 2021 the Center published a report, "Recommendations concerning help for victims of cultic influence," which contained several far-reaching ideas about ways to monitor and control such entities.[39] The report has been roundly criticized by some scholars (Creemers 2021; Fautré 2023), and Willy Fautré (2021) suggests that concern about Islam gave initial impetus to governmental efforts to exert control over minority religions. The recommendations include requirements to follow certain organizational patterns, financial arrangements, and other quite specific ideas on how minority religions should function. Fautré, as well as Creemers (2021), argue that such a wide-ranging report that affects all minority faiths is problematic and should not become official policy. It remains to be seen how, or even if, the recommendations offered will be implemented.

While the Center has engaged in its effort to develop ways to better control and manage minority religions, the courts in Belgium have demonstrated some independence from the government's position, as has been seen in Germany and France. For example, a nearly twenty-year-long battle was fought over the status of Scientology in Belgium, which involved at least two different investigations and several trials. Federal prosecutors attempted to have the organization banned, using charges of fraud, extortion, and running a criminal organization (BBC 2015). The effort was finally concluded in 2016 with the Justice Court of Brussels ruling against the Prosecutor and dismissing all charges against Scientology, with the judge stating that beliefs could not be prosecuted and that the investigations were biased (Introvigne 2016).

Three other major court cases involved the Jehovah's Witnesses. One was a case brought against a Witness congregation in Ghent because of the practice of "shunning" that is sometimes applied against members who violate important precepts and practices of the Witnesses. The Public Prosecutor in Ghent brought a case in 2015 on behalf of some former Witnesses who had been shunned by their congregation, using a 2007 antidiscrimination law that had been passed in Belgium by the Belgian government.

---

[38] www.ciaosn.be/.
[39] www.ciaosn.be/recommandation230626.pdf.

The Government prevailed at the trial court level in a decision criticized as ignoring international legal precedents on shunning and religious freedom (Richardson 2025b). This anomalous ruling was then overturned on June 7, 2022, by the Court of Appeal of Ghent, which concluded that shunning can be freely taught and practiced in Belgium (Introvigne 2022b) and the decision was then confirmed by the Belgian Court of Cassation.

A second major loss in the courts involved the massive campaign launched by the Center for Information and Advice on Harmful Cultic Organizations against the Jehovah's Witnesses for allegedly engaging in systematic child sex abuse and then concealing such crimes from authorities. This was provoked by claims made by the Center, since disproved (Introvigne 2022b), that mass media in the Netherlands had presented information about child sex abuse in Belgian Witness communities. This misinformation was presented to the Belgian Parliament, provoking a large outcry and other actions focused on discrediting Jehovah's Witnesses in Belgium. The Belgian judiciary took the accusations seriously and opened an investigation leading to the Prosecuting Judge authorizing a search of Witness headquarters in Belgium. The Court of Brussels ruled on October 5, 2021, that the charges against the Witnesses were unfounded and dismissed the case. On June 18, 2021, the Belgian Jehovah's Witnesses sued the Belgian Ministry of Justice for defamation. The Court ruled in favor of the Witnesses, but at the time of this writing, an appeal of that judgment was pending.

Belgium also suffered a significant loss in an ECtHR case involving the Witnesses. In 2001 the tax laws of Belgium were revised making it clear that religious organizations would be exempt from such taxes. Thus, Kingdom Halls for all Witness congregations in Belgium were allowed the exemption, along with many other religious groups, including of course, the predominant Catholic and Protestant denominations. However, on November 23, 2017, the law was amended to restrict the property tax exemption to nationally "recognized religions" only, which in Belgium included only Roman Catholic, Protestant, Anglican, Jewish, and Muslim national organizations. Six Witness congregations of the Jehovah's Witnesses in Brussels filed suit against the government but lost at the trial level and before the Belgian Constitutional Court. They appealed to the ECtHR, which handled the case rapidly and issued a strongly worded unanimous ruling in their favor only two years later, stating that Belgium had violated Article 9 (Freedom of Religion and Belief) and Article 14 (Discrimination).

Thus, while the Belgian government's approach seems similar to the French model of opposition to, and control of, minority religious groups, the Belgian courts, and eventually the ECtHR, have rendered judgments offering a modicum of assurance that the situation in Belgium may be somewhat ameliorated.

2 Theoretical Application to Specific Western Countries and Judicial Systems: Italy, the Netherlands, Denmark, and the United Kingdom

The book *Regulating Religion* discussed several European countries in a section called "More Tolerant European Nations" (Richardson 2004).[40] These countries, and others as well, had managed to avoid the hysteria that occurred in the United States and the moral panic that has gripped Germany, France, and Belgium. Indeed, there is a sharp contrast. How and why this significant difference occurs is worth examining, even if briefly, using available materials for the four "more tolerant" countries – Italy, the Netherlands, Denmark, and the United Kingdom.

It should be noted at the outset that all four more tolerant countries, along with many others in the pan-European region, are experiencing issues with how to integrate Islam into their societies. Some European nations have significant populations of immigrant Muslims who came in the immediate aftermath of World War II, either by invitation to help rebuild, or because of difficulties in their home country that led them to seek refuge elsewhere. In the late twentieth and early twenty-first centuries, waves of immigrants, particularly from Africa, have exacerbated the problem of integration due to racial visibility and ethnic-cultural differences. The older and newer immigrant Muslim populations can be very different historically and culturally, and these differences have contributed to concerns with incorporating them into their host societies. Moreover, the significant differences in Muslim religious practices, including domestic practices, gender issues, and dress norms, have drawn the attention of those steeped in the largely Christian-oriented cultures of Western European countries. Some politicians in Europe have made opposition to immigration a major election issue, fomenting anti-Islam sentiment among the populaces of their countries.

Handling cultural integration is made more complicated because immigrant Muslim populations are not necessarily unified within a new host country. Various Muslim groups have developed within Western European societies, often depending on the country of origin and the timing of

---

[40] This selective subset included Italy (Homer 2004), The Netherlands (Singelenberg 2004), Denmark (Rothstein 2004), and the United Kingdom (Beckford 2004b).

arrival. Various groups make valid claims to represent the most Muslims in a country and thus are able to legitimately engage in negotiations with governmental leaders. For instance, there are at least four or five Muslim groups in Italy that represent various subgroups of Muslims (Introvigne 2025), a fact that has hindered efforts to find a pathway for legal recognition and integration. A similar situation in Germany has frustrated efforts there to find a way to incorporate Muslims into the legal and normative structure of religious groups in that society (Aires, Sahinöz, and Richardson 2023). As the following discussions indicate, the influx of Muslim immigrants is challenging even more religiously tolerant societies.

Italy

Perhaps surprisingly, Italy has developed a reputation for being open and accepting of new and minority religions. Homer (2004) offers a brief history of the establishing of Italy as a nation and how interactions with the Catholic Church and some extant religious minorities – particularly the Waldensians but also some Protestant groups – contributed to this posture vis-à-vis more contemporary new faiths.[41] "Italy has become a trendsetter in creating laws and procedures that foster religious liberty in an increasingly pluralistic society" (Homer 2004, 203). Homer especially credits the modern Italian judicial system for rulings that have favored such controversial groups as Scientology, the Unification Church, and TFI. He details how these and other court rulings implement statutes enacted over the years that established methods whereby minority faiths could gain legal recognition and even financial support from the government. Those statutes have been successfully used by a large number of smaller religious groups in recent decades, although some minority religions have experienced difficulties gaining legal status.[42] In addition, no overall law granting religious freedom for minority religions has been enacted. Nevertheless, Muslim groups have had difficulty gaining official status within Italy. In general, however, the situation in Italy concerning minority religions is more favorable than that found in Germany, Belgium, and France.

---

[41] Homer credits Massimo Introvigne, well-known Italian scholar and the founder of Center for Studies on New Religions (CESNUR), for much of the information in his chapter, and he cites several publications by Introvigne (see for example Introvigne 1994, 2001a, 2001b).

[42] The Jehovah's Witnesses have made repeated efforts to gain the status granted many other minority faiths, but to no avail, leading them to file a recent claim with the ECtHR (Introvigne 2025).

The Netherlands

The Netherlands is another society in which moral panics over newer religions have not developed. Richard Singelenberg (2004) describes a society where critics of NRMs and other minority religions have made efforts to galvanize public opinion against minority faiths of various kinds. Those efforts contributed to a few sensationalized reports in the media in the Netherlands that raised public concern. However, such efforts were not ultimately successful. When the government did become concerned enough to sanction a formal report in 1984, its conclusions were innocuous and led to no further governmental action.

A more recent effort involved an unsuccessful effort by Chinese diplomats to encourage the Dutch government to limit activities and asylum opportunities for Chinese refugees, many of whom had fled religious persecution in the People's Republic of China. In addition, efforts have been made by a Dutch group affiliated with the anticult FECRIS organization[43] centered in, and financed by, France to seek sanctions against the Jehovah's Witnesses for alleged child sex abuse (HRWF 2025). The Dutch Ministry of Justice and Security commissioned a study by a Dutch university on the issue, but it was poorly done and easily critiqued by several scholars of religion, leading to no further governmental action (Introvigne 2025). It is worth noting in concluding this brief review that Singelenberg (2004), in a prescient epilogue to his report of an otherwise calm and relatively peaceful society regarding NRMs, did alert readers to a growing problem concerning assimilation of Islam into the pillarized Dutch society.[44] Singelenberg's closing comment drew attention to the growing challenges faced by the Netherlands and many other European societies about the influx of Muslims into society.

---

[43] FECRIS, the European Federation of Centres of Research and Information on Sectarianism, is a French nonprofit association and anticult organization. It serves as an umbrella organization for organizations concerned about groups considered cults or sects in Europe.

[44] At the time of Singelenberg's writing (2004), there were 450 mosques in the Netherlands. Pillarization refers to the historical organization of Dutch society into separate social groupings or "pillars," based on religion or political preference, each with its own institutions, including newspapers, bakers, trade unions, schools, and other ways of self-identification. The most prominent have been Protestant and Catholic, with a major political one organized with the Social Democrat party. Pillarization was developed in the late 1800s to manage conflict between social groups, and it served well in that regard. However, more recently support for pillarization has dissipated under various contemporary pressures, including the integration of Islam into Dutch society.

Denmark

Denmark also has avoided major controversy over NRMs and other minority faiths (Rothstein 2004, 2015), with some nuances worth noting. During the 1980s and 1990s, the country experienced a major effort to influence public opinion against NRMs. At that time, the Dialog Center International (DCI), headed by Professor of Missiology, Johannes Aagaard, issued many reports and claims that NRMs, especially Scientology, were dangerous and should be controlled. The DCI was a major countercult organization that had considerable influence in Denmark; it also had branches operating in a number of other European countries, including Germany and several in Eastern Europe. However, Aagaard retired from DCI in 2003, which contributed in part to the eventual demise of the Danish branch of DCI in 2007. The influence of the DCI lessened considerably, allowing the general culture of Danish "indifference to religion" (Rothstein 2004, 231) to return concerning NRMs. Rothstein gives some credit for this more positive atmosphere to the fact that the Ministry of Ecclesiastical Affairs and the mass media rely to a significant extent on scholars of religion for policymaking and news stories. He also was able to secure a quite positive and lengthy statement from the Minister of Ecclesiastical Affairs regarding state management of religion (Rothstein 2004, 232).

It should be noted that the DCI had focused considerable attention on Scientology, which contributed to its being denied some privileges that had been granted to many other minority faiths, for example, performing weddings and receiving tax breaks. Rothstein (2004, 226–8) offers considerable detail about Scientology's interactions with the Danish government, suggesting that it became the major focus of anticult sentiment in Denmark for a time. He also calls attention to the growing animus toward Islam in Denmark, a problem that has developed considerable momentum since his 2004 report. Since then, however, attention has been focused on a governmental investigation of alleged child sex abuse, shunning, and other activities in the Jehovah's Witnesses, following accusations made in a tabloid magazine. According to Introvigne (2024b), this was provoked by a similar development in Norway in which the government was attempting to exert control over the Witnesses. How this development will be handled by the government and the mass media is not clear at the time of this writing.

The United Kingdom

James Beckford (2004b) investigated how prisoners of different religions are treated while incarcerated in the United Kingdom. Followers of several different minority religions are represented in those institutions, including Buddhists, Sikhs, Hindus, Jews, and Muslims, although the vast majority of prisoners are either from Christian denominations or claim no religion. He notes that at the time he was writing three religions were not allowed to be registered: Rastafarianism, the Church of Scientology, and the Nation of Islam (Beckford 2004b, 241). These were designated "non-permitted religions," which violated written policies requiring nondiscrimination in the prison system. Beckford points out that the Church of England has statutory authority over prison chaplaincy, and that although some Muslims chaplains had been added, limitations remain on the religious freedom of non-Christian prisoners. Sophie Gilliat-Ray (2007), who worked with Beckford on the prison chaplain research project, offers a somewhat more optimistic interpretation as she notes that the growing presence of Muslim chaplains in UK prison systems and a similar development in the UK health system.[45]

Although Beckford's study did not address the broader UK society and treatment of minority faiths, other information suggests that, while there have been some well-publicized incidents and legal cases involving some of the controversial groups,[46] the overall atmosphere toward minority religions seems far removed from the moral panics noted in Section 1 (see Bradney 2014 for details on several cases). Examples include a ruling in 2013 by the UK Supreme Court that Scientology was in fact a religion and worthy of protections and privileges afforded other religious groups (Roux 2021, 62–3). This represents a significant shift from the British government's position some decades earlier when Scientologists were precluded from entering the country between 1968 and 1980, even if they had been offered employment there (Richardson 1995b, 52–3). A child custody dispute involving TFI in 2000 also resulted in another controversial NRM ultimately prevailing in a major High Court case (Bradney 2014; Richardson and Borowik 2026; see Section 5 of this Element).

Another indication of religious tolerance in the United Kingdom was the formation in 1988 of INFORM (Information Network Focus on Religious Movements) through the efforts of Eileen Barker, a Professor at the London School of Economics at the time.[47] This organization had

---

[45] Gilliat-Ray, Schmid, and Ali (2024) expand on the earlier work by Beckford and Gilliat-Ray to describe the growing field of Muslim Chaplaincy in Europe and the United States.

[46] Perhaps the best-known such case involved a suit filed by the Unification Church against the *Daily Mail* newspaper for some very critical articles published in 1978 concerning UC recruitment methods. This long-running legal action involved 117 witnesses, and resulted in a loss for the UC, which was ordered to pay court costs and damages. See www.nytimes.com/1981/04/01/world/moon-s-sect-loses-libel-suit-in-london.html for details.

[47] INFORM, https://inform.ac/about-us/.

as its focus the furnishing of accurate information about controversial religious groups to the media, the government, and members of the general public (Barker 2001, 2006). INFORM received funding from the British government's Home Office, from the Church of England, and other religious organizations, and has continued to operate for more than thirty-five years. It has been moved in recent years to the University of London where it is currently housed. The presence of INFORM in the United Kingdom has helped ameliorate concern about NRMs. Moreover, the organization has also served as a model for similar organizations in other countries.

The four more tolerant Western European countries discussed here share governments that function in a manner that usually offers support for religious freedom, particularly for Christian-oriented faiths. Their particular historical situation has contributed to them being able to avoid succumbing to moral panics concerning the new other minority faiths that have occurred in other European nations. Political leaders seem more attuned to concerns about religious freedom, and their judicial systems have, when needed, been able to offer support from more tolerant views toward most minority religious groups. Although minority religions have had to adjust their activities to adhere to normative and legal expectations within all the societies examined in Sections 1 and 2, they have been able to function and maintain their presence. Nevertheless, all countries have faced adjustments regarding the integration of Muslim immigrants into their societies.

3 The European Court of Human Rights

Religious freedom for minority religious groups and movements varies greatly among societies, with there being dramatic differences between societies that adhere to the rule of law and those that do not. The previous sections described those rule of law nations with relatively autonomous judicial systems. In the twenty-first century, these nations have seen courts exert their authority to protect religious freedom, a situation that has been termed the judicialization of religious freedom (Richardson 2015c).[48] However, even in those countries there is sometimes considerable change and evolution that is not always supportive of religious freedom. The "culturalization" of religion in some rule of law countries has resulted in less religious freedom for some groups and individuals as historical cultural values have become prioritized due to pressures from more traditional entities and values. This is particularly clear in France and Belgium, and to some extent in Germany. Although the European Court of Human Rights – the court of last resort

---

[48] See footnote 13 for definition of "judicialization of religious freedom."

for the 46 member nations in the Council of Europe (CoE) and an excellent example of a rule of law regional alliance – has been a counterweight to limitations of religious freedom, it too can also succumb to culturalization pressures.

The ECtHR has contributed considerably to the social construction of religious freedom in the contemporary world.[49] The Court was referred to as "semi-constitutional" (Forwein 1993) by one early member of the European Rights Commission[50] in the Court's history. Since then, its power and purview have grown, as noted by a number of scholars (e.g., Madsen 2007, 2016; Koenig 2015). Although a brief history of religious freedom in rulings of the ECtHR will be presented here, it serves primarily background for a recent major shift in jurisprudential pattern of the Court concerning religious freedom for new and minority religions.

The events of World War II led to the establishment in 1949 of the CoE, made up of a number of Western European countries. The European Convention of Rights and Fundamental Freedoms, which was drafted by the CoE in 1950, came into force officially in 1953.[51] The Convention was designed as an effort to preclude future violations of human and civil rights of European citizens such as occurred prior to and during the war. Included in the European Convention were provisions aimed at religion and the ability of citizens to practice their religion. Article 9 of the Convention specifically centered on protecting religious freedom while other articles referred to protections for religious and other groups to assemble (Article 11) and to not be discriminated against on many grounds, including religion (Article 14). Article 9 states:

1. Everyone has the right to freedom of thought, conscience and religion; this right includes freedom to change her/his religion or belief and freedom, either alone or in community with others and in public or private, to manifest her/his religion or belief, in worship, teaching, practice and observance.

---

[49] See, for example, Evans 2001; Richardson and Shoemaker 2007; Lykes and Richardson 2014; Richardson and Lee 2014; Fokas 2015a, 2015b, 2016, 2018; Richardson 2017a; Fokas and Richardson 2019; Temperman, Gunn, and Evans 2019. This Element focuses on the European Court of Human Rights because it has developed a robust, even if sometimes inconsistent, judicial history concerning religious freedom issues. It should also be noted, however, that the Court of Justice of the European Union has, in the last few years, started developing its own jurisprudence in this area. The development is similar to that of the ECtHR, but there are interesting differences (Witte and Pin, 2021; Richardson 2024, 2025b).

[50] The Commission was the precursor of the Court itself, which came into being in 1959, first as a part-time court, but later as a permanent and full-time entity (Richardson 1995b, 2017a).

[51] www.echr.coe.int/documents/d/echr/Convention_ENG.

2. Freedom to manifest one's religion or beliefs shall be subject only to such limitations as are prescribed by law and are necessary in a democratic society in the interests of public safety, for the protection of public order, health or morals, or for the protection of the rights and freedoms of others.[52]

Article 9 was ignored for some forty years after promulgation of the European Convention, with the CoE deferring to member states for regulating religious groups and activities, through development of the doctrine of "margin of appreciation."[53] In 1993, however, Greece was found in violation of Article 9 – it had statutes making proselytizing a criminal offense. The case involved a member of the Jehovah's Witnesses, Minos Kokkinakis, who had been arrested and fined for offering his testimony to the wife of a Greek Orthodox minister (Richardson 1995b, 47–8). Kokkinakis had in fact been arrested many times, as had other members of the Witnesses, whose members were the only ones ever charged under the statute that criminalized proselytizing. The ruling in that case, which might be thought of as an early "pilot judgment" of the ECtHR (Sadurski 2009; Janneke 2012), favored Kokkinakis and was critical of Greece's criminalizing of his actions. The judgment included some quite strong – and now oft-quoted – declarations concerning the importance of religious freedom for a democratic society (see Temperman, Gunn, and Evans 2019).

The actions of the ECtHR in *Kokkinakis* and subsequent numerous cases supportive of minority religions – many brought by Jehovah's Witnesses – meant that religious freedom was to be an important value in the "new Europe," and one to be protected, especially in the newer regions of the CoE that joined after the collapse of the Soviet Union (Richardson and Garay 2004; Garlicki 2007; Evans 2010). Most of those new members of the CoE did not have a history and cultural values supportive of religious freedom in a way analogous to the situation in Western Europe. They typically had a historical de jure or de facto national church with considerable power and influence, even if that religion had been suppressed during Soviet times. Religious pluralism and the attendant need for recognition of religious freedom for other faith groups was often a new concept in those

---

[52] www.echr.coe.int/documents/d/echr/Convention_ENG.
[53] "Margin of appreciation" is a term developed by the Court to refer to situations where it defers to the cultural values of the particular society from whence a case is submitted. In short, the Court decides not to intervene in certain areas where the Court is satisfied that the values of the society will produce a result that comports with values and goals of the European Convention (Fokas and Richardson 2019).

nations. *Kokkinakis* was an important step to promoting a transition to a more democratic approach to religion in those new CoE societies.

In the first two decades of the twenty-first century, however, under considerable pressure from both older and newer member CoE states, the Court has reined in its support for religious claims somewhat, especially for those brought from most early members of the CoE.[54] This has been justified in recognition of the historical and cultural values of member states, a stance adopted by the Court that has diminished the judicialization of religious freedom in the CoE (Mayrl and Venny 2021). Instead, a recently reinforced margin of appreciation doctrine (Evans 2010; Berry 2019) has contributed to a newer jurisprudential pattern, referred to above as the "culturalization" of religion (Beaman 2012–2013, 2024). The consequence of these developments is that the Court has begun to recognize and privilege traditional and historical roles of religion in some CoE societies, particularly the early members (see Fokas 2015b, 2018; Richardson 2019; Breskaya, Giordan, and Richardson 2024).

This significant change was first signaled with the dramatic reversal by a Grand Chamber decision of an original ruling by a panel of the Court in *Lautsi* v. *Italy* (see Fokas 2015a, 2015b, 2016, 2018; Breskaya, Giordan, and Richardson 2024, 32–5). The case began in a small town in Italy in 2002 when a Finnish citizen filed a complaint seeking removal of a crucifix that was on the wall of her children's school. It was heard at the local level administrative court, which referred the case to the Italian Constitutional Court in 2004, which refused to rule and returned it to the local court. That court dismissed the claim with a ruling that focused on the cultural and historical, rather than religious, meaning of the crucifix, which the court stated should not be ignored. An appeal was then filed with the Supreme Administrative Court in Italy, which accepted the historical and cultural argument made by the state and ruled against the plaintiff. She then submitted an application to the ECtHR and in 2009 received a unanimous ruling from a seven-member court section that the crucifix was predominately a religious symbol and thus its presence on the wall of a public school violated the right to an effective education, as well as Article 9 of the European Convention.

The initial decision caused a major uproar within Italy and the CoE, leading to the case being referred by the Italian State to the ECtHR's Grand Chamber for review. A number of NGOs, seventeen members of

---

[54] Greece is an exception, with several important rulings against Greece (Richardson and Garay 2004).

the CoE's Parliament, as well as ten individual CoE member nations filed interventions, with most opposing the initial decision (Fokas 2018, 10). In 2011, the Grand Chamber issued a strongly worded 16 to 1 decision favoring the Italian State's position and declaring that no violation of the Convention was found. This decision represented a major adjustment in the Court's approach to religious freedom cases after two decades of support for religious freedom (see Fokas 2016). During that time, the Court had rendered several dozen decisions supportive of minority religious groups being able to function and also for individuals to be able to practice their religion in various ways. The Court has ruled against many Muslim claimants (Meerschaut and Gutwirth 2008; Martinez-Torron 2014), although that pattern shows signs of changing in more recent decisions (Richardson 2019).

The Grand Chamber's *Lautsi* decision was a watershed moment in the history of ECtHR jurisprudence. The decision made use of a case involving religion to offer considerable deference to national and local cultural and historical considerations. This newer perspective of the Court represents a seismic shift in the jurisprudence of the Court in the area of religion and beyond and has resulted in use of the margin of appreciation doctrine to allow other rulings where CoE member states prevail in a number of cases. This new approach is particularly applied to cases from most of the early members of the CoE (Fokas 2015a, 2016; Richardson 2019, 2021b), but is not so visible in the handling of cases from newer CoE member states.[55] The *Lautsi* decision appears to be an example of a court system deliberately limiting its authority and purview voluntarily, an illustration of the dejudicialization of religious freedom (Mayrl 2018; Mayrl and Venny 2021).

4 Theoretical Application to Specific Non-Rule of Law Countries and Judicial Systems: China, Russia, and Iran

The more expansive treatment of minority religions in most European countries,[56] despite the recent shift in the ECtHR's approach to religious freedom cases, remains a stark contrast to how the court systems in a

---

[55] Fokas (2018, 10) notes that the concept of margin of appreciation is mentioned twenty-seven times in the Grand Chamber *Lautsi* decision, and eight times in the final paragraph of the ruling. See Gunn (2019) for a quite critical view of the machinations of the ECtHR as it develops a confusing jurisprudential pattern with religion cases. Also see chapters in Fokas and Richardson (2019), as well as Berry (2019) and Martinez-Torron (2016) for discussions of Article 9 jurisprudential patterns.

[56] Even in France and Germany, the court systems have a considerable degree of autonomy as shown in the discussions above of those countries.

number of other countries operate. China, Russia, and Iran, with highly centralized and pervasive governance structures, present case studies in how states manage religion in order to *limit* religious freedom. They are examples of rule by law countries that use the law to exert maximum control over all aspects of society, including religion. The situation in China will be briefly described first, followed by examinations of the situations in Russia and Iran.

China

Although China is a large country in both size and population, it is politically consolidated, with a powerful central government dominated by the Chinese Communist Party (Broy 2024). Repressive control of religious movements is challenging but has been accomplished in recent decades, and has been particularly effective with, for example, suppression of Falun Gong (Edelman and Richardson 2003, 2005; Tong 2009) and, more recently, the Church of the Almighty God (Introvigne, Richardson, and Šorytė, 2019) and the Uyghur Muslims (Palmer et al. 2021, 2024). The Falun Gong and CAG were virtually extinguished in China or driven underground, with hundreds of arrests being made of practitioners who are harshly treated when incarcerated (Tong 2009). However, both groups were able to take advantage of the pandemic chaos to expand clandestinely within China, leading to further efforts to suppress them. Efforts by the central government to control and even eradicate the Uyghur culture in Xinjian have been well documented (Human Rights Watch 2024). Harassment of many other religious and spiritual groups, including Tibetan Buddhists and the Catholic Church, also continued. In the case of the Chinese Catholic Church, this led to a decision by the Vatican to acquiesce to CCP dominance. Moreover, lawyers who try to defend minority religious groups in China are themselves subject to sanction (Human Rights in China 2001), and there are no NGOs that can effectively defend religious freedom for individuals and groups being persecuted by the State.

One major aspect of the explanation for China's success in suppressing religious freedom is that the country has no independent judicial system that might be able to ameliorate the social control efforts directed at minority faiths. Indeed, the judicial system has been actively engaged in implementing the government's plan of control and eradication, a classic example of rule by law (Edelman and Richardson 2003, 2005). This extreme situation of social control of religion exists despite guarantees of religious freedom in the Chinese Constitution. China's constitution states that its citizens enjoy "freedom of religious beliefs," and the government officially recognizes five religions: Buddhism, Catholicism, Islam, Protestantism, and Daoism. However, governmental authorities closely monitor all religious activities and even those formally recognized churches must adhere to the official policies that are an effort to remake those religious traditions into ones that grant ultimate authority to the atheistic Chinese government (PEW Research Center 2023). Considerable resources are expended by the Chinese government to monitor and control religious groups that do not adhere to the official stance on religion, as they may be viewed as competitors to the government. Such disfavored noncompliant groups can be dealt with quite severely (Yang 2006; Tong 2009).

Russia

Geographically, Russia is even larger than China, but it too is very centralized politically and has exerted pervasive control in recent decades over several religious groups, especially those considered as competitors to the Russian Orthodox Church (ROC). This includes Muslim movements, Christian ones such as the Jehovah's Witnesses, and American-derived NRMs (Shterin and Richardson 2002; Shterin 2024). It has officially abolished – or "liquidated" – some religious groups using laws against extremism passed in the aftermath of the World Trade Center destruction in 2001 (Richardson 2017c). Russia now clearly exemplifies what can occur when an officially recognized religion, the Russian Orthodox Church, forms an alliance with an autocratic political structure and uses its connections and power to attack minority religious groups while also promoting the government's agenda in other areas (Finke and Mataic 2021).

This domineering approach to religious groups that the ROC views as competitors did not occur immediately after the fall of the Soviet Union. Indeed, in the early 1990s, a new constitution was adopted with sections on religion patterned after provisions in Western-oriented governing documents; new laws were passed that implemented this orientation (Shterin 2024). There was in fact a hope and expectation of many that Russia was becoming a new member of the group of nations governed by the rule of law. After these changes in governing documents occurred there was a movement of a number of Western religious groups to come to Russia and also some, which had been operating underground, developed a more public presence as they assumed they could now promote their beliefs and practices openly.

However, this influx of newer religions, coupled with the coming out of some which had operated more clandestinely, alarmed the ROC and some governmental officials, and a backlash developed quickly. This ultimately led to the passage in 1996 of much more restrictive legislation and the ignoring of the constitutional provisions that seem to promote religious freedom in a way familiar to citizens of Western democracies (Richardson, Krylova, and Shterin 2004). New religious groups that had been registered under the provisions developed in the early 1990s were required to reregister and to operate with quite onerous provisions concerning numbers of participants and length of time functioning in Russia. Some challenges to these new provisions were initially successful in court, but it was not long before the courts adopted the official political posture, thus severely limiting religious freedoms for any Russian citizen who might express interest in a religion that was not the ROC (Shterin and Richardson 2002).

Russia has also criminalized a number of NGOs that promote human and civil rights, accusing them of being agents of foreign powers. This clear example of rule by law has further limited access to religious freedom in Russia. Russia has been a member of the CoE and had lost a number of ECtHR cases brought by Jehovah's Witnesses and some Muslim groups (Lykes and Richardson 2014). Russia refused to implement the Court's decisions, claiming national sovereignty instead. It also declined to pay its financial its obligations to the CoE, and, after the invasion of Ukraine, was expelled as a member of the CoE. Thus, Russian citizens who think their religious freedom is being violated now have no effective recourse to either Russian courts or the ECtHR.

Iran

Iran is yet another very centralized state controlled by a dominant political order based on a narrow version of Islam designed primarily to maintain control in the hands of a group of Shia clerics. The government has made many attempts to exert control over religious and spiritual ideas permeating the culture from the West (Adeliyan Tous and Richardson 2024). The version of Shia Islam promoted by the state allows little ideological flexibility, leading to severe penalties – up to and including leaders of new groups and spiritual movements being sentenced to death by a usually complicit judicial system. Such treatment of leaders of small minority religious and spiritual groups are internally justified by the assumption that they are not only misleading Iranian citizens but also are challenging the authoritarian theocratic state.

Nevertheless, the Iranian post-Revolutionary Constitution guarantees religious freedom for its citizens. Article 23 states: "The investigation of the beliefs of a person is forbidden, and no one may be molested or prosecuted for holding a belief." Also, Iranian citizens who follow certain historical religions from the region, including Zoroastrianism, Judaism, and Christianity, are granted special protections in Article 13 (Adeliyan Tous and Richardson 2024, 6). However, other provisions of the Constitution make it clear that all Iranian citizens are expected to adhere to a version of Islam promoted by political authorities in Iran. This includes the historical traditions supposedly granted special protections in Article 13, as well as any other religious or spiritual movement that might develop within Iran. The Baha'i are treated particularly poorly, with most citizenship rights barred for those who adhere to this faith (Adeliyan Tous and Richardson 2024, 19–22).

The courts in Iran have little independent authority and are expected to enforce the particular version of Islam supported by the regime, rendering harsh penalties for leaders and practitioners of any religious group or tradition deemed to be in competition with the accepted interpretation of Islam.[57] Minority faiths in Iran have in the twenty-first century been dealt with in a number of ways not strictly legally, based on the claim that they threatened the identity and unity of Iran. Moreover, discrimination against such groups has been facilitated by statutes adopted in Iran in 2021 as detailed in Adeliyan Tous and Richardson (2024, 32–45). This change in legal justification seems an indication that the government is increasingly concerned about the influx of newer religious and spiritual concepts from the West coupled by a lower level of commitment to the government sponsored version Islam (Adeliyan Tous and Richardson 2024, 24–5).

It is clear that the approach to religious freedom in China, Russia, and Iran – countries not guided by a rule of law governing philosophy – exists in sharp contrast to that of most Western nations. Those nations have adopted a rule by law perspective, and thereby severely limit religious freedom for individuals and nonsanctioned religious organizations in those nations.[58]

---

[57] This is made clear in Article 167 of the Constitution, which reads: "A judge shall be required to try to find out the verdict of every lawsuit in codified laws; if he fails to find out, he shall render a judgment on the matter under consideration based on authentic Islamic sources or authoritative fatāwā. He may not refrain from dealing with the case and rendering a judgment on the pretext of silence, inadequacy, or brevity of or contradiction in codified laws."

[58] An important point for understanding the authoritarian forms of religious control in those countries is the selective use of the ideas from Western anticult movements to

5 Law, the Courts, and "Deformation" of Minority Religions

New religious movements evolve and change over time, sometimes into entities quite different from their origins. A number of factors contribute to change in religious groups, including internal factors such as changing demographics of members; allocation of resources to family maintenance (Palmer and Hardman 1999); recruitment of different types of individuals; and a "natural" differentiation into more complex organizations as the group grows, which sometimes includes even international expansion.[59] I call the process of change "deformation" (Richardson 1985b), if change is imposed on the religious groups by forces external to them. By deformation is meant the changing of modes of organization and operating, as well as of beliefs, from those that served as the basis of the original group.

There are crucial external factors to consider that might compel changes in religious groups, including especially the law and the courts, as this section demonstrates. It is worth noting that the deformation hypothesis has many historical antecedents. For example, members of the Church of Jesus Christ of Latter-day Saints moved across the United States because of cultural differences and legal difficulties they encountered. They eventually modified their practices and even religious doctrines because of the refusal of the courts to accept their polygamous practices in the late 1800s (Bowman 2024). Groups such as the Church of Christ, Scientist that developed practices and beliefs concerning medical issues that were out of mainstream cultural values have been dealt with harshly by governmental entities and the courts (see subsection on Christian Science for discussion of use of "Spiritual Healing" instead of traditional medical care). These encounters sometimes led to dramatic changes in the groups and may have even contributed to their demise.[60]

---

promote the official positions concerning religion. A prominent anticultist from Germany testified in a major case in Moscow in defense of efforts by the Russian Orthodox Church to exert control over (or dissolve) several new and minority faiths (Shterin and Richardson 2000). French envoys and organizations have been active in China and Russia (Shterin and Richardson 2000; Edelman and Richardson 2003, 261–2; Duval 2017). In addition, ideas from some leading anticultists from the United States have been very influential in developing official policies in Iran that have led to exerting control over these newer religious movements (Adeliyan Tous and Richardson 2024, 30–1).

[59] For an excellent discussion of how NRMs change, see Barker (2013) and especially the last chapter by David Bromley (2013), which offers a useful theoretical understanding of the changes described in the volume.

[60] Efforts at social control affect the self-definition of individual participants as well. See an application of deformation theory to personal identity development and change in Central and Eastern Europe as a result of governmental efforts to suppress the new movements (Richardson 2010).

Starting in the 1970s, NRMs in the United States were criticized by families who developed a narrative claiming that their adult children had been brainwashed.[61] They persuaded news media and government agencies to "do something about these dangerous groups." When NRMs came to the attention of the mass media, in state and local legislatures, by law enforcement, and in the courts, the groups were forced to develop survival strategies and allocate resources in their defense, if they were to survive. Some, such as Scientology, and other minority religions such as the Jehovah's Witnesses, eventually had notable success in the courts in defending themselves from attacks in societies observing rule by law (Côté and Richardson 2001; Richardson 2009, 2015b, 2017c; Roux 2021). Even these more successful organizations, however, were impacted by the experience. Many other groups with less expertise and experience in dealing with legally based attacks were often impelled to modify their practices and even beliefs, sometimes drastically, in response to the external pressures being brought to bear on them. Some simply disappeared, perhaps in part because of pressures external to the group.[62]

This section examines several cases that show NRMs and minority religions defending themselves in court or using the courts themselves to promote their views and practices, and how such experiences contributed to changes within the group. It also considers the ways in which an autonomous judicial system can make rulings to encourage or even force changes in religious groups.

Changes in the Church of Scientology

While there is a wealth of scholarly literature about the development and functioning of Scientology,[63] the focus here is on legal and public relations actions involving Scientology and their effects on the organization. Several scholars have described court cases and related activities. Palmer (2008, 2009) and Westbrook (2024) detail the machinations of the

---

[61] For more on brainwashing, see Bromley and Richardson (1983); Anthony (1990); Richardson (1993b); Richardson and Introvigne (2001); Introvigne (2022a).

[62] For examples of induced change (or even liquidation) in the United States, see Lewis (1994); Wright (1995); Wright and Richardson (2011); Richardson and Bellanger (2014). For international perspectives and examples, see Richardson (2004); Marinović Jerolimov, Zrinščak, Borowik (2004); Barker (2013); Wright and Palmer (2016); Barker and Singler (2022); and Strausberg, Wright, and Cusack (2020) for changes in religious practices in Eastern and Central Europe after the fall of the Soviet Union.

[63] See Lewis (2009); Urban (2011, 2013); Westbrook (2018), Roux, (2021). Also see the special issue of *Nova Religio* 2017(1), guest edited by Regis Dericquebourg devoted to Scientology.

French government to exert control over Scientology in that country.[64] Wright and Palmer (2016, 218) have documented France's effort to control or abolish Scientology, as well as other minority faiths, including more than twenty law enforcement raids against Scientology facilities over two decades. Anson Shupe (2009) reported extensively on the battles between Scientology and the Cult Awareness Network. Scientology eventually acquired the name and other assets of CAN after the anticult group lost a major legal battle in which it was successfully sued because of an effort to deprogram a young Scientologist (Roux 2021). This writer (Richardson 2009) and Roux (2021) discuss several successful legal battles fought by Scientology in Western countries that attempted to exert control over Scientology activities or even force its dissolution. Scientology prevailed within the courts in Italy (also see Introvigne 2004), Germany, the United Kingdom, Australia, Belgium, Spain, and even France, Germany, and Russia – the latter three countries through cases brought before the European Court of Human Rights. A major legal victory for Scientology in the United States was the recognition of Scientology as a religion by the Internal Revenue Service in 1993, after many years of legal battles over the tax status of the Church.

All of these actions taken against or by Scientology demonstrate that the organization was forced to allocate considerable resources to legal and political activities – either to defend itself or to take action itself in various countries that functioned under the rule of law and had reasonably autonomous judicial systems. According to one experienced Scientology official located in Europe, Eric Roux, Church leaders learned early that it had to defend itself on many fronts in various countries. Church leaders established a specific department to deal with external affairs of all kinds and each Scientology Church has such a department, although they can vary greatly in proportional size. That department is currently called the Office of Special Affairs (OSA), which handles public relations, government affairs, and also promotes social programs sponsored by the Church, along with managing any legal action in which the individual Church is engaged. As part of efforts to defend the Church, OSA has developed considerable prowess and experience in legal matters and has been involved in various forms of litigation for nearly the entire existence of Scientology. Indeed, it has a well-earned reputation for being litigious,

---

[64] Also see Adeliyan Tous, Richardson, and Taghipour (2024) for details on French efforts to develop legal mechanisms to exert control over Scientology.

which is a tactic that may deter some critics and governmental agencies from taking actions against the Church.[65]

Roux also stressed that Scientology has learned over the years that it must abide by the laws of any country in which it operates. Thus, one major duty of the OSA is ensuring Scientology's compliance with any applicable laws. This focus on compliance may reveal areas where a country or a locale is not adhering to its own laws; this in turn has led to political and even legal efforts to force governmental compliance with its own statutes. Many current efforts of OSA are devoted to public relations and promoting humanitarian social programs sponsored by Scientology in various countries. According to Roux, because the Church has won many such battles, litigation has become less important in recent times. Scientology's right to exist in many Western societies seems to have been established, even if controversies remain in some countries.

The public relations efforts of the Church deserve special attention because of the huge internet battles in which the Church has been involved. Donald Westbrook's account (2018) describes the efforts of Church representatives to counter attacks that have been launched by detractors, many of them former members and even leaders of the Church. Although Scientology had been actively promoting its views and philosophy in social media since the inception of the internet, efforts to counter negative information online increased in this area. This development was motivated in part by the release of a large number of allegedly secret and sacred Scientology documents that had been made available on the internet. Voluminous allegedly true copies of internal Scientology documents were released in the case *United States* v. *Fishman* (743 F, Supp. 713, N. D. Cal. 1990), allowing detractors to publish them on the internet. This in turn led to a major effort for Scientology defenders to prevent and prohibit dissemination of the documents, an effort that has not been very successful (Urban 2013).[66] Westbrook (2021, 387), however, thinks the issue of whether Scientology's efforts will eventually prevail in the "internet wars" is an open question. It remains to be seen whether the allocation of resources to defend Scientology in the cyber arena will be effective. Thus, Scientology has been forced over the decades of its existence to use many of

---

[65] See Shupe (2009) and Richardson (2009) for details of the proactive litigation strategy adopted by Scientology, and see Adeliyan Tous, Richardson, and Taghipour (2024) for an example of how this stance seems to have deterred the French government from taking action against Scientology in recent years.

[66] Urban (2013, 75) also describes Scientology's major but eventually unsuccessful efforts to modify Wikipedia entries that deal with Scientology.

its resources in defensive efforts involving judicial systems. And as the battleground has shifted from the courts to the internet, in large part because of the *Fishman* case, Scientology has been allocating more resources to this new arena of activity in order the defend itself.

Changes in the Unification Church

The Unification Church (now called the Family Federation for World Peace and Unification, which I abbreviate UC), has also been a very controversial NRM, having been the subject of governmental hearings, legislative actions aimed at control, or even liquidation, and numerous legal actions against the organization in countries around the world. The considerable negative attention of legal and political authorities directed toward the UC developed because UC beliefs and practices often did not comport well with values of the dominant culture. In addition, some activities of UC members were thought to violate norms and even laws in societies where the UC was operating. Criticism focused on recruitment tactics, fundraising efforts, mass weddings, and concern about the UC attracting many young higher status recruits was widespread. As with other new and minority religions, the UC had to learn to operate within the confines of whatever legal structure was extant in a society. Alternatively, if UC leaders thought relevant statutes were not being followed or were applied unfairly, then the UC would launch challenges to those provisions, many of which were successful.[67]

The UC seems to be a classic example of the claim that NRMs are sometimes dramatically affected by governmental action and legal battles. Like Scientology, many of those legal battles have been initiated by the UC, as they defend their practices and various ways the organization operates. Mickler (2000), who reported that the UC was involved in "near constant litigation since 1975," presents a list of nearly sixty major legal actions of various types in the United States involving various UC entities and individuals and causes of action, one of which went all the way to the Supreme Court (and was successful there, although with a 5–4 margin). He also discusses specific actions taken by the UC that resulted in gaining the right to engage in public solicitation (dozens of such cases filed between

---

[67] A number of NRM scholars have written about the UC, including John Lofland (1977); Shupe and Bromley (1980); Bromley and Richardson (1983); Bromley (1988a, 1988b); and Richardson (1992). Eileen Barker's study *The Making of a Moonie: Brainwashing or* Choice (1984) was awarded the annual book award from the Society for the Scientific Study of Religion. The UC has also produced reputable scholars from within its own ranks, particularly Michael Mickler, who has written on various aspects of the Church's history, particular its legal involvements and its finances (Mickler 1987, 2000, 2013, 2021, 2022, 2024).

1977 and 1978 across the nation, with nearly all successful); the right to tax exemption privileges as a bona fide religion; to take action against deprogrammers who kidnapped UC members; to stop the expansion and misuse use of conservatorship statutes against members of the UC;[68] and to allow foreign UC missionaries to come into the United States. He also discusses twenty different government reports and hearings focused on the UC that required the organization to defend itself.

Perhaps the best-known legal action involving UC was the tax evasion trial of Rev. Sun Myung Moon (1920–2012), which resulted in his spending thirteen months in a federal prison. This much-criticized action by federal tax authorities (see H. Richardson 1984; Richardson 1992) involved a small amount of money that did not meet the usual criteria for prosecution, but the case was pursued anyway. The effort by tax authorities engendered considerable support for Rev. Moon from other religious organizations that managed their finances similarly to that of the UC. Many amicus briefs were submitted to the US Supreme Court when the case was unsuccessfully appealed, including many from large traditional religious organizations. This legal case took up considerable time and attention of the UC, and substantial resources were allocated to defend Rev. Moon and one codefendant.

The UC won a major victory in Europe after Rev. Moon was barred from entering any of the so-called "Schengen nations" (Vasmatics 2021; Zoehrer 2021).[69] However, it should be noted that the UC has achieved some success internationally in legal actions, including winning a case against Russia in the ECtHR in 2009.[70] The UC has also been the target of legal actions and governmental attacks in several countries, including efforts to ban the organization outright in various countries such as Austria, Singapore, the Republic of China, Thailand, the Philippines, and others, including most recently, Japan. The UC had been under attack in Japan since it developed there, in large part because of its Korean origins. Deprogramming of UC members was being practiced against UC members in Japan long after it had been abandoned in America and most other countries (Richardson 2011a; Duval 2025a). However, the assassination of former Prime Minister Shinzo Abe by the son of a UC follower on

---

[68] See Bromley (1983) and Mickler (1987) for more details on the conservatorship issue as it was being used for a time against NRM members, including those from the UC.
[69] The Schengen Area is comprised of twenty-nine European nations who agreed in 1985 to abolish border controls and allow the free movement of people, goods, and services within the area. It is named after the place of the signing of the agreement.
[70] www.bailii.org/eu/cases/ECHR/2009/262.html.

July 8, 2022, provoked a huge outcry against the UC and calls for its dissolution. The concerted campaign against the UC has involved efforts to pass legislation and also massive media attacks against the Church (Nakayama 2023; Duval 2025b). Duval has criticized the efforts to dissolve the UC in Japan and violations of human rights commitments to which Japan is a signatory (Duval 2024). In March 2025, a Japanese court ordered the dissolution of the Unification Church, following a request by Japan's Education Ministry. If this decision is upheld on appeal, this means that the UC will cease to exist as an organization in Japan and all its assets – buildings and bank accounts – will be given to a liquidator to become part of a fund to compensate so-called "victims" of the UC and also to pay the victims' lawyers. A decision by the appeal court is expected in late 2025.

And in September 2025, South Korean authorities arrested Hak Ja Han, the wife of the late Rev. Moon and current leader of the UC, on charges of bribery. Dealing with all of these legal actions – taken by the UC either as plaintiff or as defendant – means that a large and not inconsequential amount of UC resources were devoted to these efforts. In addition, the church had to respond to numerous governmental hearings and reports, at the national, state, and local levels. This constant battle detracted from efforts to expand the organization and promote its message.[71]

Changes in the Children of God/The Family International

The early history of the COG (now TFI) was filled with as much controversy, if not more, as that of Scientology and the Unification Church. The COG/TFI was by far the most notorious of groups that were a part of the so-called Jesus Movement. The group created parental concern because it attracted numerous young people to an itinerant lifestyle that required sending some of them off on missionary activities in over ninety countries (Davis and Richardson 1976). Their deliberate efforts to disrupt services in Christian churches, which they viewed as hypocritical, upset others. However, they were particularly reviled because the group developed practices of sexual sharing among its members and engaged in the practice known as "flirty fishing," which used sex as a recruitment tool between 1977 and 1987 (Richardson and Davis 1983).[72]

---

[71] This analysis will not deal with controversies within the UC concerning who should control UC assets after the death of Rev. Moon (see Mickler 2013). This seems a classic case of the well-known "successor crisis" that affects new religions when the founder dies (Melton 1997).

[72] Many scholars have written about this multifaceted group, including Gordon Melton (1997); William Bainbridge (2002); Claire Borowik (2013, 2014, 2023); and this author (Richardson 1994, 1999c; Richardson and Borowik 2026).

The COG/TFI has undergone many changes over time which have been well chronicled by Claire Borowik, who directed public and legal affairs for the group between 2006 and 2010. She describes continual opposition to the group by detractors and the attendant negative media treatment that eventually contributed to considerable changes in the organization (Borowik 2013). In 2010 there occurred a major "Reboot," which resulted in the discontinuation or revision of many practices and beliefs of the group, as significant efforts were made to align the organization with the dominant culture of societies in which they were operating.

Borowik (2014) also describes the many pressures brought to bear on COG/TFI organizations in various countries, including Argentina, Spain, Australia, and France in the early 1990s (also see Richardson 1999b). She details how dozens of COG homes experienced military-style raids involving hundreds of armed personnel that resulted in over 600 children being separated from their parents, some of whom were arrested. Those raids were instigated by oppositional groups, including some former members, and other entities within the so-called anticult movement who influenced government officials and mass media in those countries. The raids often featured claims of child abuse or neglect, including sexual abuse.[73] As a result, the children were forced to undergo various rigorous physical and psychological examinations and also have their educational progress assessed.[74]

The upshot of all these disruptive actions by the authorities was for all the children to eventually be returned to their parents; any parents who were incarcerated were released. However, these results occurred only after numerous and sometimes lengthy legal actions took place in which COG members were forced to defend themselves. These legal actions, of course, required the allocation of significant resources to mount defenses, thus another example of deformation of this controversial missionary-oriented group.

One other important legal action clearly demonstrates the deformation hypothesis. Richardson and Borowik (2026) offer details of the longest child custody case in UK history that took place over several years in the 1990s. The much-publicized case involved a custody dispute between a

---

[73] Charges varied greatly by country and included, in addition to claims involving children, such things as prostitution, drug possession, racketeering, kidnapping, operating an illegal school, fraud, and offending the moral order.
[74] See Wright and Palmer (2016) for more details about the raids against the COG/TFI, as well as other minority faiths in many different countries. Also see Richardson (1999a) for details about the raids in Australia.

mother within a COG group in England whose own mother sought custody of her grandchild. The over 200-page decision of Lord Justice Ward finally allowed the mother to retain custody, but only after he was assured that the organization had implemented sweeping changes in how it operated. Not only did this case involve allocation of resources to respond to charges, but it also resulted in needed changes of practices in the organization that had resulted in child sexual abuse. This decision is a clear demonstration of how legal actions can result in changes within a religious organization.[75]

Changes in Hare Krishna (ISKCON)

The International Society for Krishna Consciousness was one of the most visible and controversial of the newer religions that burst on the scene in America in the 1970s (Rochford 1985) and then spread to a number of other countries around the world. ISKCON devotees were very noticeable because of their dress and their lively public chanting. They were seen in a variety of public spaces practicing *sankirtana* (chanting the holy names of God), handing out literature, and asking for donations. These actions were challenged by authorities in various locales, but some key court cases were resolved on First Amendment grounds in ways that allowed such activities to continue. This situation was short-lived, however, as efforts by authorities developed new legal theories to justify exerting control over ISKCON activities.

Sociologist E. Burke Rochford discusses some of the early legal cases ISKCON won, such as against Los Angeles International Airport and the City of Chicago (Rochford 1988). He claims that by the mid-1970s ISKCON was functioning in every major airport in America, as well as on the streets of major cities, in national parks, and at state fairs in a number of states According to Rochford, the success in fundraising led to an emphasis on financial gain instead of the original mission of ISKCON, which was to promote the movement's philosophy and lifestyle. The success also encouraged some activities that were ethically questionable (Rochford 1988, 281–4). Thus, the early legal victories paradoxically contributed to major changes in the organization and how it functioned.

The seemingly incessant fundraising created a negative view of ISKCON in mass media and with the general public. New legal actions were filed against various ISKCON entities in the late 1970s, based in general on

---

[75] Borowik (2014) describes how the continual attacks have now moved to the internet, forcing the organization to attempt to develop some expertise in that area in order to defend itself.

claims that the way Krishna devotees were comporting themselves in their fundraising efforts did not constitute activities protected by the First Amendment. Those legal actions were eventually successful in having time, place, and manner restrictions forced on the organization, or in disallowing their activities completely (Rochford 1988, 293–5; Richardson 1998b). This new round of legal actions eventually culminated in a precedent-setting ruling by the US Supreme Court in 1981 allowing the Hare Krishnas to continue activities at the Minnesota State Fair but be limited to a booth, rather than being able to circulate through the crowds at the fair.

These legal losses contributed to a growing disillusionment among Hare Krishna devotees. Some members had started families and were no longer living communally in ashrams; thus they were obliged to find ways to support their families. After the death of Swami Prabhupada in 1977, an internal conflict among various factions in the movement ensued – a "succession crisis" (Melton 1997). The leadership crisis was in part a consequence of a scandal that developed over child abuse within boarding schools set up within ISKCON facilities to take care of children so their parents could go into public places to practice *sankirtana*, to raise funds, and to support themselves.

These boarding schools, called *gurukulas*, operated in the late 1970s into the 1980s in various places around the United States and abroad. Former students charge the *gurukulas* of fostering child abuse of various kinds, including sex abuse (Rochford 2007; Burt 2023; Nilsson 2024). Sensationalized media coverage of the abuses contributed greatly to negative perceptions of ISKCON in the United States. In 2000, a lawsuit seeking $400 million in damages was filed in Federal Court in Dallas, Texas on behalf of several dozen former students at various *gurukulas*. A federal court dismissed the suit, which was then refiled in a Texas State Court, with several dozen additional plaintiffs. This lawsuit resulted in declarations of bankruptcy by several ISKCON communities named in the suit. By the time matters were settled in bankruptcy court, more than 500 former students were listed as plaintiffs. They were collectively awarded $9.5 million dollars, to be distributed according to the types of abuse and length of time endured by the claimants.

One result of these various issues is that ISKCON temples around America and elsewhere were forced to find other ways to maintain themselves. They did so by appealing to what Rochford (2007, 2013) refers to as the "Hinduisation" of ISKCON. This term refers to deliberate efforts by various ISKCON entities to attract the growing number of Hindu citizens who had immigrated from India and Nepal to the United States. These efforts were reasonably successful, and most temple communities were able to survive, but have become vastly different in character, as Rochford (2018) describes in some detail. The original enthusiasm of young, first generation, devotees has evolved into a style of worship with some similarities to congregational life in other more traditional religions. Thus, the ISKCON experience with the law and attendant media attention has led to widespread changes in the movement.

Changes in Christ Communal Organization

For a brief time, the Christ Communal Organization, another Jesus Movement group, operated in Oregon (Harder, Richardson, and Simmonds 1972; Richardson, Harder, and Simmonds, 1979). Centered at a rural facility referred to as "The Land," CCO engaged in agriculture as one method to support its communal lifestyle. The group was unusual in that it did not use street solicitation as a method of fundraising (Richardson 1988, 28–9). Instead, it produced much of its own food needs, and generated funds from sales of produce from The Land and other agricultural projects in the area that it owned and operated. The organization also developed work teams that were hired out to do agricultural work for other farms, for example, picking fruit, harvesting vegetables, and especially tree planting for a large timber company. The proceeds from such efforts went directly to the organization instead of to individual workers. This method resulted in an adequate means of support for several years, and the group was able to maintain itself and even develop other outposts in a number of states across the United States as well in a few foreign countries.

Initially CCO had received approval from the Internal Revenue Service (IRS) to operate as a tax-exempt organization, thus relieving it of paying taxes on proceeds from sales of products and also from the proceeds of the work teams that were hired out to other agricultural entities in the region. However, this situation was not to last, as in the mid-1970s the IRS changed its position and sent CCO a tax bill for well over a million dollars (see Richardson and Sim 1982). The IRS justified this change of definition by claiming that CCO was operating as a religious organization as a subterfuge, and that it was really functioning as a money-making entity with the proceeds accruing to the benefit of group leaders. This and other efforts by governmental entities forced changes in practices, and even beliefs, of this Jesus Movement organization (Stewart and Richardson 1999). The position taken by the IRS with CCO has been roundly criticized by some prominent tax attorneys (Emory and Zelenak 1982) who became defenders of CCO in the ensuing legal battles with the IRS. Emory and Zelenak pointed out that the IRS was discriminating against NRMs such as CCO. They noted that the Catholic Church, for example, had been granted a nation-wide exemption for its operations, some of which were similar in functioning to that of CCO.[76]

The failure of legal efforts to defend CCO's method of operating and supporting itself led to the demise of the movement. Indeed, The Land property and other assets were eventually assumed by defense attorneys as payment for their legal services. CCO members who resided on The Land and other communal operations eventually left, with some departing the group completely. However, many members folded into various Calvary Chapel churches that were developing around the country at that time (see Richardson 1993a). Thus, the demise of the communal operations of CCO because of IRS legal action had a major impact on the growth of Calvary Chapel over the next few years. The dramatic changes in CCO exemplify how governmental decisions and subsequent legal actions can lead to the deforming and even demise of a religious organization.

Changes in the Church of Christ, Scientist

Although the Church of Christ, Scientist is not considered a controversial NRM, it has been embroiled in considerable controversy in the past over its use of spiritual healing, especially in regard to medical treatment for children of Church members. Many other Christian-oriented groups also practice versions of spiritual healing. Monica Miller (2014, 228) lists over a dozen religious groups that practice some form of spiritual healing derived from interpretations of selected passages in the Bible. Christian Science is by far the best known of such groups and has been responsible for major efforts to gain exemptions in federal and state laws to allow use of spiritual healing in cases involving children where traditional medical interventions might seem indicated (Miller 2014, 229).

Changing sentiments concerning child welfare have resulted in heightened awareness of child morbidity and mortality in the various groups practicing spiritual healing. Some states have ignored statutes that granted exemptions for spiritual healing and some states have changed their statutes to no

---

[76] I became involved in this case at the request of the group since I had been doing research on them for years (Harder, Richardson, and Simmonds, 1972). I offered expert testimony that took issue with the claim that this was not a religious group deserving of tax-exempt status. One result was that attorneys for the IRS subpoenaed all my research data, a disturbing effort that was eventually rebuffed by CCO's attorneys who convinced the judge that this was simply a "fishing expedition" designed to intimidate CCO and myself.

longer offer an exemption. Cases involving Christian Science have attracted considerable critical attention to the Church and it practices, and its earlier successful efforts to gain exemptions in federal and state laws have come under attack. These efforts by state authorities forced the Church to allocate more resources to legal defense of members who have been prosecuted for child endangerment, child abuse, and even manslaughter. In addition, changes have occurred in the way such cases are handled by the Church as well as other relevant matters (Richardson and DeWitt 1992).

The modifications that have occurred are instructive from the perspective of the deformation thesis. One major operational change was for the national Christian Science organization to start managing legal cases that arose instead of maintaining some distance from them. That initial posture forced individuals and their congregations to defend as best they could when accused of violating laws related to the death of a child. This sometimes resulted in badly managed cases and considerable negative publicity. The centralization of case management, of course, required a reallocation of resources in order to implement the new approach.

Even more interesting are changes in the Church's position on how to define the situations involving a child needing medical care, some of which suggest changes in the beliefs of the Church. Changes included:

(1) emphasize that parents, not Church authorities, are to make decisions about welfare of a child with a medical condition;
(2) urge parents to examine their own spiritual context and strength and that of their family and friends as they consider how to proceed when dealing with a child's medical problem;
(3) state that even if parents decide to seek medical treatment for a child's illness they will remain in fellowship with the Church; and
(4) Church members are directed not to ostracize parents who decide to seek medical treatment for their child. (Richardson and DeWitt 1992, 561)

It is worth noting that the above elements were not considered to be restatements of Church positions by Church officials. However, those statements do suggest that Church practices and even underlying ideas were adjusted in trying to deal with the aftermath of the controversy over how CS children in need of medical care were dealt with.[77]

---

[77] When Church officials reviewed the draft of the Richardson and DeWitt article, they stressed that there were no major changes in practice or beliefs, and that the Church had simply issued a restatement of beliefs and practice issues in 1991 in an effort to clarify to members and the general public what Church policies were regarding medical treatment for children.

Changes in Jehovah's Witnesses

Jehovah's Witnesses, which emerged in the late nineteenth century in the United States, are a fascinating example of how involvement in legal actions can change a religious organization.[78] They were the first religious organization to which the deformation thesis was applied (Côté and Richardson 2001). Their involvement in the legal arena led to thoroughgoing changes not only in their operation and functioning but also in the culture and even some beliefs of the organization. Such transformations were somewhat ironic, given that Witnesses do not participate in politics, do not vote, do not serve on juries, and do not defer to secular authorities.

Côté and Richardson (2001) describe two major efforts the Witnesses undertook to use courts in the United States and elsewhere to defend and promote their beliefs and practices, both of which were characterized as a "disciplined litigation" approach.[79] The first such effort occurred in the 1930s and 1940s, with a number of cases filed with courts across the country addressing the right to proselytize and other matters, such as refusing to salute the flag and refusing military service through conscientious objection. Many of these cases eventually reached the US Supreme Court, which ruled in the Witnesses' favor in a number of cases. In two such cases – the controversy over saluting the flag and the fees imposed for distributing literature – the Supreme Court actually reversed earlier judgments against Witness practices and issued new rulings affirming them. In the middle decades of the twentieth century, the Witnesses won dozens of cases accepted by the Supreme Court, which led to a disbanding of the Church's legal arm for a time.

This lull in legal actions was not to last. The second major use of litigation concerned how the Witnesses would defend their abstention from blood transfusions, a doctrine that was formally adopted in 1961. Because many in the medical profession ignored this religious prohibition, the Jehovah's Witnesses filed a number of cases across the country in the 1970s to gain legal sanction for their beliefs. This return to disciplined litigation successfully persuaded the courts to allow refusal of transfusions, and to require damages when such health directives declared by adults were ignored by medical professionals. In more recent times the

---

[78] See Beckford (1975) for an excellent sociological assessment of the development of the Witnesses. Also see Manwaring (1962); Zygmunt (1975); Penton (1979); McAninch (1987); Kaplan (1989); Voas (2007); Brace (2014); Richardson (2015b, 2017c); Chryssides (2016); and Chu and Peltonen (2024).

[79] Disciplined litigation refers to a strategy of carefully selecting legal actions to undertake in terms of the issues concerned, the forum in which to submit them, and the likelihood of a favorable outcome. Also, it involves very careful and thorough preparation of any legal actions that are undertaken, with the matter being undertaken by very experienced attorneys.

Witnesses have had to defend themselves in several countries against charges of various kinds of child abuse, as recounted in some of the reports on individual countries discussed earlier, as well as in Japan.[80]

This orientation toward reconstituting the organization into one attentive to litigation when needed then evolved into what Côté and Richardson call "vigilant litigation." This term refers to an approach that views litigation as a tactic to be used selectively. The vigilant litigation approach is currently being tested in several countries that are seeking control or dissolution of the Witnessed based on allegations of child sex abuse or because of their practice of "shunning" members who violate some major tenet of the group.[81] Legal attacks that seem to be coordinated have been launched in the Czech Republic, Norway, Belgium, Spain, New Zealand, and Denmark, among other countries. Most of the litigation has been thwarted by courts and governmental entities that accepted information and testimony from some scholars of religion quite knowledgeable about Witness practices. Nevertheless, the Witnesses have lost a few cases, for example, New Zealand, while others are ongoing. The Jehovah's Witnesses have also made considerable use of the European Court of Human Rights, once it began to start enforcing European Convention provisions supportive of religious freedom. They have submitted several hundred cases from various countries throughout Europe and have achieved a very impressive record of wins with that Court (Richardson 2015b, 2017c, 2025a).[82]

Côté and Richardson (2001) conclude that the vigilant litigation strategy offers a model for newer controversial religions to use in defending themselves and their practice and beliefs. They suggest that Scientology and the Unification Church in particular might find such an approach useful. It is clear that these groups and other minority faiths have indeed used such an approach and been successful doing so, at least in nations that operate under the rule of law.

---

[80] In Japan the issue of treatment of children in the Witnesses arose out of concern about the UC after the Shinzo Abe assassination. Some opposed to the Witnesses used this event as an opening to attack the Witnesses, using claims of child abuse to promote the campaign. This led to a large research project developed by the Witnesses and some academics whose research focused on the organization. A preliminary report of findings from this research was presented in fall of 2024 at a professional conference (Richardson, Wright, and Barker 2024).

[81] See Chu and Peltonen (2024, 42–5) regarding changes in Jehovah's Witnesses practices in this regard.

[82] As reported in Richardson (2025a), the record achieved so far by the Witnesses with the ECtHR includes 140 cases with favorable outcomes, with 103 favorable judgments, 27 "friendly settlements," and 10 "unilateral declarations" (where governments accede to the Witness claims). There are several dozen cases pending before the Court so this record probably will continue to grow.

This section has shown how new and minority religions have adapted and even altered beliefs and practices because of the confrontation with opponents in the courts and in the court of public opinion. The analysis is offered as a corrective to explanations that emphasize internal factors and broader political and cultural considerations as reasons for alterations in minority religious groups. Several prominent examples from selected controversial minority religious groups presented earlier demonstrate how court decisions sometimes dramatically influence and shape a religion.

6 Courts Using Minority Religions to Accomplish Their Own Agendas

This section presents a quite different perspective on the relationship of courts and minority religions. Instead of focusing on what happens to minority religious groups when they are engaged in legal actions, the thrust of this section is on what happens to the courts themselves through those interactions. Have cases involving minority religions contributed to changes in judicial systems, and if so, what was the logic justifying such actions by the courts? Details of what has occurred with the judicial systems in rule of law nations will be used to demonstrate the truth of the claim that courts may have deliberately accepted and used minority religion cases to increase their own impact (see Richardson 2017b).

Sir Ivor Richardson, former Chief Justice of the New Zealand Supreme Court, wrote insightfully about the role and responsibilities of courts (I. Richardson 1995). His ideas offer a theoretical underpinning for this section on the way various courts sought to extend their purview and authority. He was concerned about the emphasis on "rights talk" for individual liberty in contemporary societies to the exclusion of other concerns. He noted that rights talk in his home country and Australia has evolved into concern about group rights, a reference to the growing awareness of the need to take more seriously the claims of indigenous peoples in both societies. Sir Richardson supports this shift, but laments that the dual focus on individual and group rights means "relatively little emphasis is put on community rights" (1995, 2). He says:

> Living in a community entails acceptance of the community's interests and values. Individual and group rights have to be balanced with community rights.... No man is an island. Freedom of speech is not a license to defame, nor does it entitle anyone without cause to cry "Fire" in a crowded theater. Freedom of religion may be modified in the public interest by other values so as to exclude polygamy or the practice

of certain religious beliefs. Freedom of assembly does not preclude the adoption of anti-riot laws. Numerous other examples could be given of legitimate constraints on individual and group freedoms which membership of an ordered society entails. (I. Richardson 1995, 16)

Sir Richardson then proceeds to develop at some length his conception of the responsibility of the courts (I. Richardson 1995, 18–19), noting that when other means of dealing with conflicts, issues of resource distribution, and recognition of individual or group rights, are not functional, the courts must assume an important role on behalf of community rights. His argument meshes well with the concept of the "judicialization of politics" that has developed in political science and other disciplines (Tate and Vallinder 1995; Hirschl 2011), as well as with the more specific concept of the judicialization of religious freedom that has emerged within sociology of religion (Fokas 2015a; Richardson 2015c, 2021b). These concepts emphasize the role of the courts in managing difficult questions in a society, including those dealing with religion, an area of growing importance in increasingly pluralistic contemporary societies. This newly expanded role for court systems has developed because other branches of government either choose not to exercise authority on a controversial matter, or because other branches cannot agree on an issue and thus leave it to the courts to resolve in societies with a functioning tripartite system of governance.

The thrust of Justice Richardson's argument is that courts must take care to protect community rights and prerogatives even as they attempt to balance those concerns against individual and group rights, as well as other germane considerations. The community rights perspective offers a way to understand some of the decisions that courts have made as they dealt with cases involving religion discussed in this Element. It should be emphasized that Justice Richardson was writing from the perspective of a society that lives under a rule of law regime, and that his proposals are only applicable in a society that has a relatively autonomous judicial system with considerable independent authority. Certain conditions, particularly the autonomy of the courts, must be present if a court system is to promote its view of community values within the areas within its purview.

Herein I will briefly discuss how the actions of the judicial systems discussed earlier have made use of cases involving minority religions to promote their view of community values at the same time they were extending their own authority.[83]

---

[83] One other ingredient is crucial if a court wants to support community values – willing and well-prepared plaintiffs who bring strong and well-argued cases to the courts that

United States Supreme Court

The First Amendment to the US Constitution reads as follows:

> Congress shall make no law respecting an establishment of religion, or prohibiting the free exercise thereof; or abridging the freedom of speech, or of the press; or the right of the people peaceably to assemble, and to petition the government for a redress of grievances.

Perhaps surprising to some, it should be noted at the outset that the many protections codified in the First Amendment to the US Constitution were *not* initially applicable to state and local governments. Those provisions applied only to laws and policies promulgated by the Federal Government. Development of the jurisprudential pattern that resulted in provisions of the First Amendment applying also to state and local legislation and policies seems a good example of a community rights perspective being implemented by the US Supreme Court. The process whereby those important provisions were made applicable to nonfederal governmental entities is referred to as "incorporation" (Richardson and McGraw 2019, 14–15). This term is dependent on the "due process clause" of the Fourteenth Amendment, which was the mechanism whereby the Supreme Court over several decades applied First Amendment protections to nonfederal entities. That clause is included in this portion of the Fourteenth Amendment of the US Constitution:

> No State shall make or enforce any law which shall abridge the privileges or immunities of citizens of the United States; nor shall any State deprive any person of life, liberty, or property, without due process of law; nor deny to any person within its jurisdiction the equal protection of the laws.

The "incorporation" of the several protections included in the First Amendment arose through a number of cases decided by the Court in the mid-twentieth century. Furthermore, a number of those cases were brought to the Court by minority religions of one kind or another. Through their legal actions those groups were trying to defend their right to enjoy religious freedom for their members and to ensure that the groups themselves could continue to exist. Apparently, the Court developed a desire to extend

---

address issues of concern to the court (Richardson 2017b, 21). A corollary to the need to have willing and experienced plaintiffs is support and assistance from others for cases brought by willing plaintiffs. Donald Black's concept of "third party partisans" (Black and Baumgartner 1999) is a useful way to categorize NGOs and others who might have an interest in such cases. See Richardson (2017b, 2021c) for fuller discussion of this phenomenon.

the values and protections expressed in the First Amendment to all citizens in the nation. This series of decisions can be viewed as an expression of a particular set of values by the Court through its decision-making authority. These decisions seemed to reflect the belief that the nation might suffer harm if citizens could be treated significantly differently, depending on which governmental entity was impinging on their lives. To ensure similar treatment for citizens throughout the land appears to be an underlying theme of the jurisprudential pattern developed by the Court as it made a series of decisions using minority religion cases that extended the protections of the First Amendment to all residents of the United States (Richardson 2015b).

European National Court Systems

The importance of the independence of judicial systems is demonstrated with what has been happening in European national courts. Even in countries with national policies critical of NRMs and other minority religious groups, including Germany, France, and Belgium, the national court systems have demonstrated some respect for such groups in the jurisprudential patterns developed in recent decades. Belgian courts have rejected claims again the Jehovah's Witnesses, and in Germany, although it took a long time, the Constitutional Court finally ruled definitively in favor of the Witnesses being registered as a public corporation. Even in France some local courts have ruled in favor of some NRMs, such as Scientology. In the more tolerant European nations, new religions have seen fewer legal challenges, and when they have arisen, as in Italy and the United Kingdom, the courts have usually shown support for NRMs and other minority religious groups. This, of course, does not mean that every challenge to the religious freedom of minority groups has been rebuffed. There are ongoing problems associated with the integration of Islam within many European countries. However, the overall jurisprudential pattern in European nations supportive of the rule of law has been one that recognizes constitutional and statutory provisions supportive of religious freedom, where they exist.

Those extant constitutional and statutory provisions have been relied on by judges who demonstrated some respect for the importance of protecting religious minorities as they concerned themselves with their view of the overall good of society. Similarly to what occurred with major rulings in the United States, this pattern seems to demonstrate Sir Ivor Richardson's concept that the judiciaries in European countries have acted in a manner protective of a specific value perspective developed over time in Western European nations. And, as in the United States, the use of rulings in legal cases brought by (or against) minority religious groups to express that value seems clear.

European Court of Human Rights

The ECtHR offers another demonstration of Sir Ivor Richardson's theory that autonomous courts can, if allowed by underlying governing documents and not deterred by other political or institutional structures, make rulings extending their authority and purview in ways supportive of particular rights and values. The European Convention of Human Rights and Fundamental Freedoms, approved after the devastation and demonstrated inhumanity of WWII, furnished the statutory authority for the ECtHR to operate and make decisions supportive of human and civil rights. And as former Soviet-dominated nations joined the CoE, the Court began making rulings that exerted authority over those former Soviet nations.

Those rulings presented different and more stringent standards of review for newer members of the CoE, and this dual pattern seems to have continued, as noted by a number of scholars (Evans 2010; Cali 2018; Jusic 2018; Richardson 2019; Stiansen and Voeten 2019). While there may be several reasons for this dual pattern to have developed,[84] the pattern could be viewed as demonstrating the Court's desire to extend its authority to encourage the dissemination of values extant in Western European communities into the newer regions of Central and Eastern Europe whose nations have chosen to join the CoE. The Court's major shift of jurisprudential pattern that began with *Lautsi* described earlier has led, among other things, to less focus on how religion is managed in most of the CoE's early member countries. This suggests that the Court is willing to allow considerable margin of appreciation to those nations (Berry 2019) for cases involving religion (as well as other matters), but less so with newer members of the CoE. It remains to be seen whether the Court's efforts to promote values from Western European communities to all areas within its purview will be successful, or if the tensions apparent in this dual approach will lead to difficulties for the Court.[85]

---

[84] Evans (2010) compares cases dealing with individual religious freedom and dress norms (most from original CoE members) with those from newer members focused on protection of group interests and basic survival. She agrees that geography and newness (to CoE) are important considerations but also notes other reasons the rulings differ, including that the two types of cases vary greatly in complexity, with group survival cases being much simpler from a legal perspective.

[85] It should be obvious that Sir Richardson's concept of the courts preserving and promoting community values, including religious freedom, are not applicable to non-rule of law

Conclusions

This Element offers a socio-legal interpretation of three interrelated foci that, taken together, help our understanding of the meaning and effects of the many legal actions taken against, and by, newer religious groups as well as older minority faiths. It first looked at how new and older minority faiths are dealt with in legal/judicial systems in selected countries and in the European context with the ECtHR. Second, it looked at how these encounters with the legal systems have changed those religious groups in sometimes dramatic ways. Finally, it described how courts have accepted and used cases involving new and other minority religions to expand their own geographic purview and authority.

Summary

The Introduction offered a sociologically oriented analysis of how judicial systems operate in societies governed by the rule of law. Section 1 included the United States as a case study to offer some contrast with how various European countries handle minority religions. The United States has been for most of its relatively short history a federalized system operating with a tripartite governance structure. This has left considerable authority with individual states, while also allowing the court systems of the federal government and the states a great deal of autonomy and independence. Over time, however, increasing authority has accrued to the federal government, with some of that upsurge attributed to court cases involving minority religions through which protections afforded by the US Constitution have been extended to individuals and entities in the individual states. Those protections afforded by incorporating First Amendment provisions dealing with religion have contributed to a society that has offered considerable protections for religious freedom for most religious groups.

The more stringent approaches to minority faiths in Germany, France, and Belgium derive from their unique histories and cultures that contribute to contemporary concern about the growth of such groups, many of them imported from the United States. Although the governments in these three countries have promoted an approach to minority religions that attempts to control and even dissolve them, nevertheless the relative

---

societies such as China, Russia, and Iran, whose courts are dominated by political regimes that disallow any autonomy to their judicial systems. There was a brief period after the collapse of the Soviet Union when the courts in Russia did demonstrate some independence, with the Constitutional Court issuing some rulings favorable to minority faiths. This period was short-lived, however, as the government refused to honor those rulings (Richardson, Krylova, and Shterin 2004).

autonomy of the courts in those nations has afforded most minority religions some degree of protection, demonstrating again the importance of the autonomy of judicial systems for protecting religious freedom.

The Western European countries covered in Section 2 – Italy, the Netherlands, Denmark, and the United Kingdom – have been more tolerant of minority faiths. They have all managed to avoid the moral panics that occurred in the three nations covered in Section 1, which have shown less tolerance of minority groups. This is not to say that no concerns have been manifested about minority faiths, but rather that when issues did arise, the reactions were somewhat muted by governments that have not adopted a throughgoing anti-minority faith perspective. Moreover, the courts of these countries have issued rulings favoring religious freedom when cases have come to their attention.

Section 3 looked at the role and record of the European Court of Human Rights concerning religious freedom for individuals and groups concerning religious freedom. This very important regional court has built an impressive record on religious freedom issues, particularly since the fall of the Soviet Union and the influx of many former Soviet-dominated nations into the CoE. It has particularly addressed the right of minority religions to exist and function in those new member societies that lack a history of religious freedom. However, the Court has developed a split jurisprudential pattern that grants most original members of the CoE considerable leeway in how they manage religion. Indeed, in the last decade this more lenient approach with early CoE members has expanded considerably.

Section 4 focused on three nonwestern societies – China, Russia, and Iran – which all have very centralized and pervasive governmental systems that do not operate as rule of law societies. Instead, they are dominated completely by a political party, or a political party that has formed an alliance with a specific religious perspective and organization. This brief look at such autocratic and even theocratic societies demonstrates again the importance of having some degree of autonomy for the judicial systems. When that is absent, religious freedom has no champion, and the citizens are deprived of rights granted in other societies that do adhere to some version of rule of law governance.

Section 5 examined whether legal actions involving minority religious groups, whether brought against or by the group, changed or "deformed" those groups in ways that deterred them from implementing their original visions of how they should function. Such interactions with the legal and judicial systems can lead to changes in religious practices and even beliefs, as was demonstrated. A number of more controversial and well-known minority religions and newer faiths were described in detail to demonstrate the efficacy of the deformation hypothesis. This examination revealed that a variety of thoroughgoing changes had indeed been wrought by the involvement of groups with the legal systems and courts in various countries in which they were present. This result was seen with contemporary NRMs, including the Church of Scientology, the Unification Church, the COG/TFI, Hare Krishna, Christ Communal Organization (another large Jesus Movement group), and older minority religious groups such as Christian Science and Jehovah's Witnesses. Not only were ways of functioning and practices modified through engagement with legal and judicial systems, but sometimes belief systems were modified as well.

Section 6 focused on the courts themselves, to understand how courts operate and what the courts might be trying to accomplish with their rulings in the area of religion, particularly cases dealing with new or older minority religions. The analysis revealed the efforts by some court systems to expand their authority into new areas of law and geography not covered in their original remit. This expansion occurred because of efforts by judicial officials to promote Western "community values." This involved major growth of the purview and authority of both national and a major regional court, the ECtHR, as they sought to promote values that judicial leaders thought best for a given society or region. The effects of pressures on the courts from other institutional entities within a given society or region also were examined to explain how the agenda of a court system might be affected as they dealt with various cases, including those involving religion.

Final Observations

The major conclusion that can be drawn from the discussions of individual nations and regional courts demonstrates the extreme importance of an independent judiciary in order to protect religious freedom. In rule of law countries, even if they become caught up in moral panics, the courts, if supported by foundational documents granting religious freedom, can and have served as a bulwark against extreme measures being taken against minority faiths. In rule by law nations, however, the acquiescence of the courts to dominant political entities results in few if any protections for religious expression. Thus, there is clearly a strong connection between judicial independence and the rule of law, and this has great implications for religious freedom as well as other matters. This connection raises an important question of how to protect judicial independence.[86] Religious freedom is impossible without a strong judiciary willing to defend the rule of law.

It is also evident that religious groups operating within a society must do so in a manner that comports with the laws and cultural values of that society. Religious groups are changed as they encounter the legal and judicial systems in societies in which they operate. If a religious group brings a legal action themselves, they are implicitly agreeing to abide by the court's ruling, which might mean changes will be required. If they are before the courts as defendants, then the court has great power to bring about major modifications with its rulings, as demonstrated in this Element.

Finally, it is clear that judicial systems, if protected from interference by founding documents and tradition, can act in ways that extend their ability to work their will on a society – or even an entire region, as with the European Court of Human Rights. And if those founding documents include the concept of religious freedom, the courts can and have used such cases to greatly expand religious freedom, as well as their geographic purview and authority.

---

[86] Halliday, Karpik, and Feeley (2007) present strong arguments about the importance of the legal profession's attorneys and judges serving as a bulwark for the development of liberal democracies. Graver (2025a) presents evidence of disturbing trends in some former Soviet-dominated nations of how judges may succumb to pressures from political powers in states governed by autocratic regimes.

References

Adeliyan Tous, S. and J. T. Richardson. 2024. *Managing Religion and Religious Changes in Iran: A Sociolegal Analysis*. Cambridge: Cambridge University Press.

Adeliyan Tous, S., J. T. Richardson, and A. Taghipour. 2023. "Using Law to Limit Religious Freedom: The Case of New Religious Movements in France." *Religions* 14: 887. www.mdpi.com/2077-1444/14/7/887.

Adrian, M. 2016. *Religious Freedom at Risk: The EU, French Schools, and Why the Veil Was Banned*. London: Springer.

Aires, W., C. Sahinöz, and J. T. Richardson. 2023. "Trial and Error: Muslims and Shari'a in the German Context." In A. Possamai, J. T. Richardson, and B. S. Turner, eds., *The Sociology of Shari'a*, 221–37. Cham, Switzerland: Springer.

Altglas, V. 2010. "Laïcité is What Laïcité Does: Rethinking the French Cult Controversy." *Current Sociology* 58: 489–510.

Anthony, D. 1990. "Religious Movements and Brainwashing Litigation: Evaluating Key Testimony." In T. Robbins and D. Anthony, eds., *Gods We Trust*, 295–344. New Brunswick, NJ: Transaction Books.

Anthony, D. and T. Robbins. 2004. "Pseudoscience Versus Minority Religions: An Evaluation of the Brainwashing Theories of Jean-Marie Abgrall." In J. T. Richardson, ed., *Regulating Religion: Case Studies from around the Globe*, 127–50. New York: Kluwer.

Bacquet, S. 2012. "Religious Freedom in a Secular Society: An Analysis of the French Approach to Manifestations of Beliefs in the Public Sphere." In P. Cumper and T. Lewis, eds., *Religion, Rights, and Secular Society*, 147–68. Cheltenham, UK: Edward Elgar.

Bainbridge, W. 2002. *The Endtime Family: The Children of God*. Albany: State University of New York Press.

Bánkuti, M., G. Halmai, and K. L. Scheppele. 2013. "Hungary's Illiberal Turn: Dismantling the Constitution." *Journal of Democracy* 21, no. 3: 138–45.

Barker, E. 1984. *The Making of a Moonie: Brainwashing or Choice*. London: Basil Blackwell.

Barker, E. 2001. "INFORM: Bringing the Sociology of Religion to the Public Space." In P. Côté, ed., *Chercheurs de dieux dans l'espace public – Frontier Religions in Public Space*, 21–34. Ottawa: University of Ottawa Press.

Barker, E. 2006. "What Should We Do about the Cults? Policies, Information and the Perspective of INFORM." In P. Côté and T. J. Gunn, eds., *The New Religious Question: State Regulation or State Interference? (La nouvelle question religieuse: Régulation ou ingérence de l'État?)*, 371–95. Brussels: Peter Lang.

Barker, E., ed. 2013. *Revisionism and Diversification in New Religious Movements*. Burlington, VT: Ashgate.

Barker, E. and J. T. Richardson, eds. 2021. *How Minority Religions React to the Law: Case Studies and Theoretical Applications*. London: Routledge.

Barker, E. and B. Singler. 2022. *Radical Transformations of Minority Religions*. London: Routledge.

BBC. 2015. "Scientologists in Brussels Court on Fraud Charges." British Broadcasting Company, Oct. 26. www.bbc.com/news/world-europe-34638721.

Beaman, L. 2012–2013. "Battles over Symbols: The 'Religion' of the Minority Versus the Culture of the Majority." *Journal of Law and Religion* 28, no. (1): 67–104.

Beaman, L. 2024. "Religion to Culture: Who Is the 'Us'?" *Cultural Studies* 38, no. 5: 750–71. https://doi.org/10.1080/09502386.2024.2364902.

Beckford, J. A. 1975. *The Trumpet of Prophecy: A Sociological Analysis of Jehovah's Witnesses*. Oxford: Blackwell.

Beckford, J. A. 1985. *Cult Controversies: The Societal Response to the New Religious Movements*. London: Tavistock.

Beckford, J. A. 2004a. "'Laïcité,' 'Dystopia,' and the Reaction to New Religious Movements in France." In J. T. Richardson, ed., *Regulating Religion: Case Studies from around the Globe*, 27–40. New York: Kluwer.

Beckford, J. A. 2004b. "Social Justice and Minority Religions in Prison: The Case of England and Wales." In J. T. Richardson, ed., *Regulating Religion: Case Studies from around the Globe*, 237–42. New York: Kluwer.

Beckford, J. A. and J. T. Richardson. 2007. "Religion and Regulation." In J. A. Beckford and J. Demerath, eds., *The Sage Handbook of the Sociology of Religion*, 396–418. London: Sage Publications.

Benhalim, R. 2019a. "The Case for American Muslim Arbitration." *Wisconsin Law Review* 2019, no. (3): 531–91.

Benhalim, R. 2019b. "Religious Courts in Secular Jurisdictions: How Jewish and Islamic Courts Adapt to Societal and Legal Norms." *Brookland Law Review* 84: 745–800.

Berger, M., ed. 2013. *Applying Shari'a in the West: Facts, Fears and the Future of Islamic Rules on Family Relations in the West*. Leiden: Leiden University Press.

Berry, S. 2019. "Avoiding Scrutiny: The Margin of Appreciation and Religious Freedom." In J. Temperman, J. Gunn, and M. Evans, eds., *The European Court of Human Rights and the Freedom of Religion or Belief: The 25 Years since Kokkinakis*, 103–27. Leiden: Brill.

Besier, G. 2018. "Jehovas Zeugen in Deutschland." In G. Besier and K. Stoklosa, Jehovas Zeugen in Europa. *Geschichte und Gegenwart*, 129–268. Berlin: LIT Publisher.

Besier, G. and R. M. Besier. 2000. "Jehovah's Witnesses Request for Recognition as a Corporation under Public Law." *Journal of Church and State* 43, no. (1): 35–48.

Black, D. 1976. *The Behavior of Law*. New York: Academic Press.

Black, D. 1998. *The Social Structure of Right and Wrong*, rev. ed. New York: Academic Press.

Black, D. and M. P. Baumgartner. 1999. "Toward a Theory of the Third Party." In D. Black, ed., *The Social Structure of Right and Wrong*, rev. ed., 95–124. New York: Academic Press.

Bogdan, H. 2011. "Explaining the Murder-Suicides of the Order of the Solar Temple: A Survey of Hypotheses." In J. R. Lewis, ed., *Violence and New Religions*, 133–45. Oxford: Oxford University Press.

Borowik, C. 2013. "The Family International: Rebooting for the Future." In E. Barker, ed., *Revisionism and Diversification in New Religious Movements*, 15–30. Burlington, VT: Ashgate.

Borowik, C. 2014. "Courts, Crusaders, and the Media: The Family International." In J. T. Richardson and F. Bellanger, eds., *Legal Cases, New Religious Movements, and Minority Faiths*, 3–23. Burlington, VT: Ashgate.

Borowik, C. 2023. *From Radical Jesus People to Virtual Religion: The Family International*. Cambridge: Cambridge University Press.

Bowman, M. 2024. *Mormonism*. Cambridge: Cambridge University Press.

Brace, T. 2014. "Jehovah's Witnesses and the Law: 'Caesar's Things to Caesar, but God's Things to God'." In E. Barker and J. T. Richardson, eds., *Reactions to the Law by Minority Religions*, 37–57. London: Routledge.

Bradney, A. 2014. "Legal Cases." In G. Chryssides and B. Zeller, eds., *The Bloomsbury Companion to New Religious Movements*, 179–93. London: Bloomsbury.

Breskaya, O., G. Giordan, and J. T. Richardson. 2024. *A Sociology of Religious Freedom*. Oxford: Oxford University Press.

Bromley, D. G. 1983. "Conservatorships and Deprogramming: Legal and Political Prospects." In D. G. Bromley and J. T. Richardson, eds., *The Brainwashing/Deprograming Controversy: Sociological, Psychological, Legal and Historical Perspectives*, 267–93. Lewiston, NY: Edwin Mellen Press.

Bromley, D. G. 1988a. "Economic Structure and Charismatic Leadership in the Unification Church." In J. T. Richardson, ed., *Money and Power in the New Religions*, 335–63. Lewiston, NY: Edwin Mellen Press.

Bromley, D. G. 1988b. "The Economic Structure of the Unification Church." In J. T. Richardson, ed., *Money and Power in the New Religions*, 305–33. Lewiston, NY: Edwin Mellen Press.

Bromley, D. G. 2013. "Changing Vision, Changing Course: En-visioning/Re-visioning and Concentration/Diversification in NRMs." In Eileen Barker, ed., *Revisionism and Diversification in New Religious Movements*, 247–60. Burlington, VT: Ashgate.

Bromley, D. G. and J. T. Richardson. 1983. *The Brainwashing/Deprograming Controversy: Sociological, Psychological, Legal and Historical Perspectives*. Lewiston, NY: Edwin Mellen Press.

Broy, N. 2024. "China and Taiwan." Religious Minorities Online. Berlin: De Gruyter. https://doi.org/10.1515/rmo.20855518.

Broyde, M. J. 2017. *Religious Arbitration in America and the West Sharia Tribunals, Rabbinical Courts, Christian Panels*. Oxford: Oxford University Press.

Burt, A. 2023. *Hare Krishna in the Twenty-First Century*. Cambridge: Cambridge University Press.

Cali, B. 2018. "Coping with Crisis: Whither the Variable Geometry in the Jurisprudence of the European Court of Human Rights." *Wisconsin International Law Journal* 35, no. 2: 237–76.

Chambliss, W. 1979. "On Lawmaking." In W. Chambliss and M. Zatz, eds., *Making Law: The State, the Law, and Structural Contradictions*, 3–35. Bloomington: Indiana University Press.

Chambliss, W. 1993. "Making Law". In W. Chambliss and M. Zatz, eds., *Making Law: The State, the Law, and Structural Contradictions,* 1–35. Bloomington: Indiana University Press.

Chemerinsky, E. 2025. "'The Playbook of a Dictator': Trump's War of Retribution on America's Legal System." *The Sacramento Bee*, March 31, reprinted in www.charlotteobserver.com/opinion/article303175486.html#storylink=cpy.

Chryssides, G. D. 2016. *Jehovah's Witnesses Continuity and Change*. New York: Routledge.

Chu, J. and O. Peltonen. 2024. *Jehovah's Witnesses*. Cambridge: Cambridge University Press.

Cohen, S. 1972. *Folk Devils and Moral Panics*. London: Granada Press.

Cohen, S. 2002. *Folk Devils and Moral Panics*, 3rd ed. London: Routledge.

Côté, P. and J. T. Richardson. 2001. "Disciplined Litigation and 'Deformation': Dramatic Changes in Jehovah's Witnesses." *Journal for the Scientific Study of Religion* 40, no. 1: 11–25.

Creemers, J. 2021. "The Flemish Draft Law on Religious Communities: A Critical Analysis." *Bitter Winter*, June 3.

Davis, D. 2000. "Religious Prosecutions in Today's Germany: Old Habits Renewed." In D. Davis, ed., *Religious Liberty in Northern Europe in the Twenty-first Century*, 105–24. Waco, TX: J. M. Dawson Institute of Church-State Studies.

Davis, R. and J. T. Richardson. 1976. "The Organization and Functioning of the Children of God." *Sociological Analysis* 37, no. 4: 321–39.

Davis, S. 2020. "Rise of French Laïcité: French Secularism from the Reformation to the Twenty-First Century." Evangelical Missiological Society Monograph Series. Eugene, OR: Pickwick.

Dericquebourg, R. 2017. "The French Law of 1905 Founding 'Laicite' and Religious Freedom." *Religion – Staat – Gesellschaft* 18, no. 1–2: 67–82.

Duval, P. 2017. "Anti-sect Movements and State Neutrality: The Case of FECRIS (European Federation of Centers of Research and Information on Sectarianism)." *Religion – Staat – Gesellschaft* 18, no. 1–2: 133–46.

Duval, P. 2024. "Japan and the Unification Church: Violation of Japan's International Commitments." *Bitter Winter*, September 28.

Duval, P. 2025a. "Deprogramming Unification Church Children in Japan: A New Plan." *Bitter Winter*, March 4.

Duval, P. 2025b. "Unification Church in Japan: A Religious Liberty Crisis That Needs Urgent Attention." *Bitter Winter*, March 8.

Duvert, C. 2004. "Anti-cultism in the French Parliament: Desperate Last Stand or an Opportune Leap Forward? A Critical Analysis of the 12 June, 2001 Act." In J. T. Richardson, ed., *Regulating Religion: Case Studies from around the Globe*, 41–52. New York: Kluwer.

Edelman, B. and J. T. Richardson. 2003. "Falun Gong and the Law: Development of Legal Social Control in China." *Nova Religio* 6, no. 2: 312–31.

Edelman, B. and J. T. Richardson. 2005. "Imposed Limitations on Freedom of Religion in China and the Margin of Appreciation Doctrine: A Legal Analysis of the Crackdown on the Falun Gong and Other 'Evil Cults.'" *Journal of Church and State* 47, no. 2: 243–67.

Emory, M. and L. Zelenak. 1982. "The Tax Exempt Status of Communitarian Organizations: An Unnecessary Controversy." In T. Robbins, ed., *Cults, Culture and the Law*, 1085–1112. Chico, CA: Scholars Press.

Evans, C. 2001. *Freedom of Religion under the European Convention on Human Rights*. Oxford: Oxford University Press.

Evans, C. 2010. "Individual and Group Religious Freedom in the European Court of Human Rights: Cracks in the Intellectual Architecture." *Journal of Law and Religion* 26: 321–43.

Fautré, W. 2021. "Flemish Law on Religion: Dangerous for Religious Freedom." Bitter Winter, August 6. https://bit.ly/3cnnoU8.

Fautré, W. 2023. "Some Reflections about the Recommendation of the Federal Cult Observatory on "Cult Victims." Human Rights Without Frontiers, October 7. https://hrwf.eu/belgium-some-reflections-about-the-recommendations-of-the-federal-cult-observatory-on-cult-victims-i/.

Finke, R. and D. R. Mataic. 2021. "Reconciling State Promises and Practices: Constitutional Promises and Discrimination against Religious Minorities." *Social Compass* 68, no. 3: 301–20.

Fokas, E. 2015a. "Directions in Religious Pluralism in Europe: Mobilizations in the Shadow of European Court of Human Rights Religious Freedom Jurisprudence." *Oxford Journal of Law and Religion* 4: 54–74. https://doi.org/10.1093/ojlr/rwu065.

Fokas, E. 2015b. "Sociology at the Intersection between Law and Religion." In S. Ferrari, ed., *Routledge Handbook of Law and Religion*, 59–75. New York: Routledge.

Fokas, E. 2016. "Comparative Susceptibility and Differential Effects on the Two European Courts: A Study of Grasstops Mobilizations around Religion." *Oxford Journal of Law and Religion* 5: 541–74. https://doi.org/10.1093/ojlr/rww050.

Fokas, E. 2018. "Religious American and Secular European Courts, or Vice-Versa? A Study of Institutional Cross-Pollination." In T. Hjelm, ed., *Peter Berger and the Sociology of Religion: 50 Years after the Sacred Canopy*, 135–55. London: Bloomsbury.

Fokas, E. and J. T. Richardson. 2019. *The European Court of Human Rights and Minority Religions: Messages Generated and Messages Received*. London: Routledge.

Forwein, J. A. 1993. "The Impact of the European Convention on Human Rights in the European Legal System." Paper presented at the 28th Legal Convention, Law Council of Australia. Hobart, Tasmania, 30 September.

Fox, J. 2020. *Thou Shalt Have No Other Gods before Me: Why Governments Discriminate against Religious Minorities*. Cambridge: Cambridge University Press.

Fox, J. 2021. "What Is Religious Freedom and Who Has It?" *Social Compass* 68, no. 3: 321–41.

Garlicki, L. 2007 "Collective Aspects of Religious Freedom: Recent Developments in the Case Law of the European Court of Human Rights." In A. Sajo, ed., *Censored Sensitivities: Free Speech and Religion in a Fundamentalist World*, 217–33. The Hague: Eleven International Publishing.

Gilliat-Ray, S. 2007. "From 'Visiting Minister' to 'Muslim Chaplain'; The Growth of Muslim Chaplaincy in Britain, 1970–2007." In E. Barker, ed., *The Centrality of Religion in Social Life: Essays in Honour of James A. Beckford*, 145–57. Burlington, VT: Ashgate.

Gilliat-Ray, S., H. Schmid, and M. Ali. 2024. "Mapping Muslim Chaplaincy: An Analytic Review of Publications between 1989 and 2023." *Journal of Muslims in Europe* 14: 1–30.

Graver, H. P. 2015. *Judges Against Justice on Judges When the Rule of Law Is under Attack*. Cham, Switzerland: Springer.

Graver, H. P. 2025a. "Judges Under Stress and the Duty to Resist." Vervassungsblog: On Matters Constitutional, March 14.

Graver, H. P. 2025b. "The Legal Battle Over Liberal Democracy." ExpertForum: Law and Policy Analysis, March 25. www.acslaw.org/expertforum/the-legal-battle-over-liberal-democracy/.

Gunn, J. 2019. "'Principle of Secularism' and the European Court of Human Rights: A Shell Game." In J. Temperman, J. Gunn, and M. Evans, eds., *The European Court of Human Rights and the Freedom of Religion or Belief: The 25 Years since Kokkinakis*, 465–573. Leiden: Brill.

Hall, J. R. 1987. *Gone from the Promised Land: Jonestown in American Cultural History*. New Brunswick, NJ: Transaction Books.

Halliday, T., L. Karpik, and M. Feeley, eds. 2007. *Fighting for Political Freedom: The Legal Complex and Political Liberalism*. London: Bloomsbury.

Hamilton, M. 2003. "Federalism and the Public Good: The True Story Behind the Religious Land Use and Institutionalized Persons Act." *Indiana Law Journal* 78, no. 1: 311–61.

Hamilton, M. 2005. *God versus the Gavel: Religion and the Rule of Law*. Cambridge: Cambridge University Press.

Harder, M., J. T. Richardson, and R. Simmonds. 1972. "The Jesus People." *Psychology Today* 6: 45–50, 110–13.

Hirschl, R. 2011. "The Judicialization of Politics." In R. Goodin, ed., *The Oxford Handbook of Political Science*, 253–74. Oxford: Oxford University Press.

Homer, M. 2004. "New Religions in the Republic of Italy." In J. T. Richardson, ed., *Regulating Religion: Case Studies from around the Globe*, 203–12. New York: Kluwer.

Human Rights in China. 2001. "Empty Promises – Human Rights Protections and Chinese Criminal Procedure Law in Practice." www.hrichina.org/en/file/2843/hric-empty-promisesc5d0.pdf?token=-3lW-uwNHAuTD9vqvkDv1doFv6d-it_lLtE1IF-Phag.

Human Rights Watch. 2024. "China: Religious Regulations Tighten for Uyghurs." www.hrw.org/news/2024/01/31/china-religious-regulations-tighten-uyghurs.

Human Rights Without Frontiers. 2025. "France: When State-funded Anti-cult Groups Think They are Above the Law," January 3. https://hrwf.eu/france-when-state-funded-anti-cult-groups-think-they-are-above-the-law/.

Introvigne, M. 1994. "Anti-cult and Counter-cult Movements in Italy." In A. Shupe and D. Bromley, eds., *Anti-Cult Movements in Cross-Cultural Perspective*, 171–97. New York: Garland.

Introvigne, M. 2001a. "Italy's Surprisingly Favorable Environment for Religious Minorities." *Nova Religio* 4, no. 2: 275–80.

Introvigne, M. 2001b. "Religious Minorites in Italy: Legal and Political Problems." *Religion – Staat – Gellschaft* 2: 127–40.

Introvigne, M. 2004. "Holy Mountains and Anti-Cult Ecology: The Campaign against the Aumist Religion in France." In J. T. Richardson, ed., *Regulating Religion: Case Studies from around the Globe*, 73–83. Leiden: Kluwer.

Introvigne, M. 2016. "All Charges Dropped against Scientology in Belgium Landmark Decisions." www.cesnur.org/2016/scientology_bruxelles.htm.

Introvigne, M. 2021a. "French Law on Separatism: 'Yes, But' Says Constitutional Council. *Bitter Winter*, August 19. https://bitterwinter.org/french-law-on-separatism-yes-but-says-constitutional-council/.

Introvigne, M. 2021b. "Jehovah's Witnesses Win Important Case in Belgium." *Bitter Winter*, October 25.

Introvigne, M. 2022a. *Brainwashing: Reality or Myth?* Cambridge: Cambridge University Press.

Introvigne, M. 2022b. "European Court of Human Rights: Belgium Found Guilty of Tax Discrimination Against the Jehovah's Witnesses." *Bitter Winter*, April 11.

Introvigne, M. 2022c. "Ghent Decision Overturned on Appeal: Jehovah's Witnesses' Shunning Can Be Freely Taught and Practiced in Belgium." *Bitter Winter*, June 20.

Introvigne, M. 2024a. "France: The New Anti-Cult Law Denounced to the Constitutional Council." *Bitter Winter*, April 17.

Introvigne, M. 2024b. "Is Something Rotten in the State of Denmark? A Strange Case Against the Jehovah's Witnesses." *Bitter Winter*, October 9.

Introvigne, M. 2025. Personal communication by email, January 1.

Introvigne, M., J. T. Richardson, and R. Šorytė. 2019. "Would the Real Article 300 Please Stand Up? Refugees from Religious Movements Persecuted as Xie Jiao in China: The Case of the Church of Almighty God." *The Journal of CESNUR* 3, no. 5: 3–86.

Janneke, G. 2012. "The Pilot Judgment Procedure Before the European Court of Human Rights as an Instrument for Dialogue." In P. Popelier and M. ClaesIntersentia, eds., *Constitutional Conversations*. Available at SSRN: https://ssrn.com/abstract=1924806.

Jusic, A. 2018. "Dammed If It Doesn't and Dammed If It Does: The European Court's Margin of Appreciation and the Mobilizations around Religious Symbols." *University of Pennsylvania Journal of International Law* 39, no. 3: 561–614.

Kaplan, W. 1989. *State and Salvation: Jehovah's Witnesses and Their Fight for Civil Rights*. Toronto: University of Toronto Press.

Koenig, M. 2015. "The Governance of Religious Diversity in the European Court of Human Rights." In J. Boulden and W. Kymlicka, eds., *International Approaches to Governing Ethnic Diversity*, 51–78. Oxford: Oxford University Press.

Kuru, A. 2009. *Secularism and State Policies Toward Religion: The United States, France, and Turkey*. Cambridge: Cambridge University Press.

LeMoult, J. 1983. "Deprogramming Members of Religious Sects." In D. G. Bromley and J. T. Richardson, eds., *The Brainwashing/Deprograming Controversy: Sociological, Psychological, Legal and Historical Perspectives*, 234–57. Lewiston, NY: Edwin Mellen Press.

Lewis, J. R. 1994. *From the Ashes: Making Sense of Waco*. Lanham, MD: Rowman and Littlefield.

Lewis, J. R. 2009. *Scientology*. Oxford: Oxford University Press.
Liptak, A. 2025. "Will Religion's Remarkable Winning Streak at the Supreme Court Continue?" New York Times, March 30. www.nytimes.com/2025/03/30/us/politics/supreme-court-religion.html.
Lofland, J. 1977. *Doomsday Cult: A Study of Conversion, Proselytization and Maintenance of Faith*. New York: Irvington.
Lykes, V. and J. T. Richardson. 2014. "The European Court of Human Rights, Minority Religions, and New Versus Original Member States." In J. T. Richardson and F. Bellanger, eds., *Legal Cases, New Religious Movements and Minority Faiths*, 171–201. Burlington, VT: Ashgate.
Madsen, M. 2007. "From Cold War Instrument to Supreme European Court: The European Court of Human Rights at the Crossroads of International and National Law and Politics." *Law & Social Inquiry* 12: 137–59.
Madsen, M. 2016. "The Challenge of Authority of the European Court of Human Rights: From Cold War Legal Diplomacy to the Brighton Declaration and Backlash." *Law and Contemporary Problems* 79: 141–78.
Manwaring, D. R. 1962. *Render Unto Ceasar: The Flag Salute Controversy*. Chicago: University of Chicago Press.
Marinović Jerolimov, D., S. Zrinščak, and I. Borowik, eds. 2004. *Religion and Patterns of Social Transformation*. Zagreb: Institute for Social Research.
Martinez-Torron, J. 2014. "Islam in Strasbourg: Can Politics Substitute for Law?" In C. Durham, R. Torfs, D. Kirkham, and C. Scott, eds., *Islam, Europe, and Emerging Legal Issues*, 19–61. Burlington, VT: Ashgate.
Martinez-Torron, J. 2016. "European Convention on Human Rights." In G. Robbers and C. Durham, eds., *Encyclopedia of Law and Religion*, 173–85. New York: Brill.
Mayer, J.-F. 1996. *Les Mythes du Temple Solaire*. Geneva: George Editeur.
Mayrl, D. 2018. "The Judicialization of Religious Freedom: An Institutional Approach." *The Journal for the Scientific Study of Religion* 57: 514–30.
Mayrl, D. and D. Venny. 2021. "The Dejudicialization of Religious Freedom?" *Social Compass* 68, no. 3: 342–58.
McAninch, W. S. 1987. "A Catalyst for the Evolution of Constitutional Law: Jehovah's Witnesses in the Supreme Court." *University of Cincinnati Law Review* 55: 997–1077.

McGraw, B. 2003. *Rediscovering America's Sacred Ground: Public Religion and Pursuit of the Good in Pluralistic America*. Albany: State University of New York Press.

McGraw, B. and J. T. Richardson. 2020. "Religious Regulation in the United States." In P. Djupe, M. Rozell, and T. Miller, eds., *Oxford Encyclopedia of Politics and Religion*, 1443–67. New York: Oxford University Press.

Meerschaut, K. and S. Gutwirth. 2008. "Legal Pluralism and Islam in the Scales of the European Court of Human Rights: The Limits of Categorical Balancing." In E. Breams, ed., *Conflicts between Fundamental Rights*, 51–66. Antwerp: Intersentia.

Melton, G. 1997. "When Prophets Die: The Succession Crisis in New Religions." In T. Miller, ed., *When Prophets Die: The Postcharismatic Fate of New Religious Movements*, 1–12. Albany: State University of New York Press, 1991.

Mickler, M. 1987. "Government Documents." In *The Unification Church in America: A Bibliography and Research Guide*, 209–13. New York: Garland Press.

Mickler, M. 2000. "Legal Gains." In *40 Years in America: An Intimate History of the Unification Church, 1959–1999*, 272–84. New York: HSA Publications.

Mickler, M. 2013. "The Post-Sun Myung Moon Unification Church." In E. Barker, ed., *Revisionism and Diversification in New Religious Movements*, 47–63. Burlington, VT: Ashgate.

Mickler, M. 2021. "No Stranger to Litigation: Court Cases Involving the Unification Church/Family Federation in the United States." In E. Barker and J. T. Richardson, eds., *Reactions to the Law by Minority Religions*, 79–96. London: Routledge.

Mickler, M. 2022. *The Unification Church Movement*. Cambridge: Cambridge University Press.

Mickler, M. 2024. "Legal, Financial, Religious and Political Issues at Stake in the Struggle Over the Unification Church's Corporate Status in Japan." *The Journal of CESNUR* 8: 111–27.

Miller, M. 2014. "Parents Use of Faith Healing for Their Children: Implications for the Legal System and Measuring Community Sentiment." In J. T. Richardson and F. Bellanger, eds., *Legal Cases, New Religious Movements and Minority Faiths*, 227–44. Burlington, VT: Ashgate.

Moore, R. 2022. *Peoples Temple and Jonestown in the Twenty-first Century*. Cambridge: Cambridge University Press.

Nakayama, T. 2023. "Why the Unification Church Should Not Be Dissolved. The Witch Hunt Should Be Stopped." *Bitter Winter*, September 22.

Nilsson, S. 2024. *Children in New Religious Movements*. Cambridge: Cambridge University Press.

Ollion, E. 2013. "The French 'War on Cults' Revisited: Three Remarks on an On-going Controversy." In D. Kirkham, ed., *State Responses to Minority Religions*, 121–35. Burlington, VT: Ashgate.

Palmer, S. J. 2008. "France's 'War on Sects': A Post-9/11 Update." *Nova Religio* 11, no. 2: 104–20.

Palmer, S. J. 2009. "The Church of Scientology in France: Legal and Activist Counterattacks in France in the 'War on Sectes'." In J. R. Lewis, ed., *Scientology*, 295–321. Oxford: Oxford University Press.

Palmer, S. J. 2011. *The New Heretics of France: Minority Religions, La République and the Government-Sponsored "War on Sects*. New York: Oxford University Press.

Palmer, S. J. 2022. "Recent Applications of France's 2001 'Brainwashing Law': Case Studies of 'Gourous' Accused of Abus de Faiblesse." Paper presented at Annual Meeting of European Association for the Study of Religion, Cork, Ireland, June 27–July 1.

Palmer, S. J. and C. E. Hardman. 1999. *Children in New Religions*. New Brunswick, NJ: Rutgers University Press.

Palmer, S., D. Mahmut, and A. Udun. 2024. *Uyghur Women Activists in the Diaspora: Restorying a Genocide*. London: Bloomsbury.

Palmer, S. J., M. Melanson, D. Mahmut, and A. Udun. 2021. "The Uyghurs in the Diaspora in Canada." *Journal of the Council for Research on Religion* 3, no. 1. https://doi.org/10.26443/jcreor.v3i1.60.

Penton, M. J. 1979. "Jehovah's Witnesses and the Secular State." *Journal of Church and State* 21, no. 1: 55–72.

PEW Research Center. 2023. "10 Things to Know about China's Policies on Religion." October 23. www.pewresearch.org/short-reads/2023/10/23/10-things-to-know-about-chinas-policies-on-religion/.

Possamai, A., J. T. Richardson, and B. S. Turner. 2014. *Legal Pluralism and Shari'a Law*. London: Routledge.

Richardson, H. 1984. *Constitutional Issues in the Case of Reverend Moon*. New York: Edwin Mellen Press.

Richardson, I. 1995. "Rights Jurisprudence – Justice for All?" In P. Joseph, ed., *Essays on the Constitution*, 61–83. Oxford: Butterworths. Available online at https://ssrn.com/abstract=2250800.

Richardson, J. T. 1985a. "The Active Versus Passive Convert: Paradigm Conflict in Conversion/Recruitment Research." *Journal for the Scientific Study of Religion* 24: 163–79.

Richardson, J. T. 1985b. "The 'Deformation' of New Religions: Impacts of Societal and Organizational Factors." In T. Robbins, W. Shepherd, and J. McBride, eds., *Cults, Culture, and the Law*, 163–76. Chico, CA: Scholars Press.

Richardson, J. T. 1985c. "Psychological and Psychiatric Studies of New Religions." In L. Brown, ed., *Advances in Psychology of Religion*, 209–23. New York: Pergamon Press.

Richardson, J. T. 1988. "Financing the New Religions." In J. T. Richardson, ed., *Money and Power in the New Religions*, 23–43. Lewiston, NY: Edwin Mellen Press.

Richardson, J. T. 1991. "Reflexivity and Objectivity in the Study of Controversial New Religions." *Religion* 21: 305–18.

Richardson, J. T. 1992. "Public Opinion and the Tax Evasion Trial of Reverend Moon." *Behavioral Sciences & the Law* 10, no. 1: 53–64.

Richardson, J. T. 1993a. "Mergers, 'marriages,' Coalitions, and Denominationalization: The Growth of Calvary Chapel." *SYZYGY: Journal of Alternative Religion and Culture* 2: 205–23.

Richardson, J. T. 1993b. "A Social Psychological Critique of 'Brainwashing' Claims about Recruitment to New Religions." In J. K. Hadden and D. G. Bromley, eds., *Handbook of Cults and Sects in America*, 75–97. Greenwich, CT: JAI Press.

Richardson, J. T. 1994. "Update on 'The Family:' Organizational Change and Development in a Controversial New Religious Group." In J. R. Lewis and J. G. Melton, eds., *Sex, Sin, and Slander: Investigation the Family/Children of God*, 27–40. Stanford, CA: Center for Academic Publication.

Richardson, J. T. 1995a. "Legal Status of Minority Religions in the United States." *Social Compass* 42, no. 2: 249–64.

Richardson, J. T. 1995b. "Minority Religions, Religious Freedom, and the Pan-European Political and Judicial Institutions." *Journal of Church and State* 37, no. 1: 39–59.

Richardson, J. T. 1996. "Sociology and the New Religions: 'Brainwashing', the Courts, and Religious Freedom." In P. Jenkins and S. Kroll-Smith, eds., *Witnessing for Sociology: Sociologists in Court*, 115–34. Westport, CT: Praeger.

Richardson, J. T. 1998a. "The Accidental Expert." *Nova Religio* 2, no. 1: 31–43.

Richardson, J. T. 1998b. "Law and Minority Religions: 'Positive' and 'Negative' Uses of the Legal System." *Nova Religio* 2: 93–107.

Richardson, J. T. 1999a. "The Religious Freedom Restoration Act: A Short-lived Experiment in Religious Freedom." In D. Guinn, C. Barrigar, and K. Young, eds., *Religion and Law in the Global Village*, 142–64. Atlanta, GA: Scholars Press.

Richardson, J. T. 1999b. "Social Control of New Religions: From 'Brainwashing' Claims to Child Sex Abuse Accusations." In S. Palmer and C. Hardman, eds., *Children in the New Religions*, 172–86. New Brunswick, NJ: Rutgers University Press.

Richardson, J. T., ed. 2004. *Regulating Religion: Case Studies from around the Globe*. New York: Kluwer.

Richardson, J. T. 2006a. "Religion, Constitutional Courts, and Democracy in Former Communist Countries." *The Annals of the American Academy of Political and Social Science* 603: 129–38.

Richardson, J. T. 2006b. "The Sociology of Religious Freedom: A Structural and Socio-Legal Analysis." *Sociology of Religion* 67: 271–94.

Richardson, J. T. 2007. "Religion, Law, and Human Rights." In P. Beyer and L. Beaman, eds., *Religion, Globalization, and Culture*, 407–28. Boston: Brill.

Richardson, J. T. 2009. "Scientology in Court: A Look at Some Major Cases from Various Nations." In J. R. Lewis, ed., *Scientology*, 283–94. Oxford: Oxford University Press.

Richardson, J. T. 2010. "Identity Theories, Religious Groups, and the Effects of Legal Social Control in Central and Eastern Europe." In I. Borowik and M. Zawita, eds., *Religious Identities in Transition*, 15–31. Krakow: Nomos.

Richardson, J. T. 2011a. "Deprogramming: From Private Self-help to Governmental Organized Repression." *Crime, Law, and Social Change* 55: 321–36.

Richardson, J. T. 2011b. "The Social Construction of Legal Pluralism." *Democracy and Security* 7, no. 4: 390–405.

Richardson, J. T. 2015a. "Contradictions, Conflicts, Dilemmas, and Temporary Resolutions: A Sociology of Law Analysis of Shari'a in Selected Societies." In A. Possamai, J. T. Richardson, and B. S. Turner, eds., *The Sociology of Shari'a*, 303–24. Cham: Springer.

Richardson, J. T. 2015b. "In Defense of Religious Rights: Jehovah's Witness Legal Cases around the World." In S. Hunt, ed., *Handbook of Global Contemporary Christianity: Themes and Developments in Culture, Politics, and Society*, 285–307. New York: Brill.

Richardson, J. T. 2015c. "Managing Religion: The Judicialization of Religious Freedom." *Journal for the Scientific Study of Religion* 54, no. 1: 1–19.

Richardson, J. T. 2016. "Law and Social Control of Religion." In D. Yamane, ed., *Handbook of Religion and Society*, 485–502. New York: Springer.

Richardson, J. T. 2017a. "The European Court of Human Rights: Changes and Challenges in the Social Construction of Religious Freedom." *Religion – Staat – Gesellschaft* 1–2: 13–34.

Richardson, J. T. 2017b. "Managing Religion: Courts as 'Partners' and 'Third Party Partisans' in the Social Construction of Religious Freedom." *Religioni e Societa – Religions and Human Rights Special Issue* 32: 13–19.

Richardson, J. T. 2017c. "Update on Jehovah's Witness Cases before the European Court of Human Rights: Implications of a Surprising Partnership." *Religion, State & Society* 45: 232–48.

Richardson, J. T. 2019. "Religious Freedom in Flux: The European Court of Human Rights Grapples with Ethnic, Cultural, Religious, and Legal Pluralism." *Changing Societies and Personalities* 3, no. 4: 303–18.

Richardson, J. T. 2021a. "The Ghent Jehovah's Witness Decision: Anomaly or a New Reality? *The Journal of CESNUR*, April 24.

Richardson, J. T. 2021b. "The Judicialization of Religious Freedom: Variations on a Theme." *Social Compass* 68, no. 3: 375–91.

Richardson, J. T. 2021c. "Minority Religions Respond to the Law: A Theoretical Excursus." In E. Barker and J. T. Richardson, eds., *Reactions to the Law by Minority Religions*, 221–35. London: Routledge.

Richardson, J. T. 2022. "Comparing Two Major Court Systems in Europe on the Matter of Religious Dress." Canopy Forum. https://canopyforum.org/2023/01/24/comparing-the-two-major-courts-systems-in-europe-on-the-matter-of-religious-dress/.

Richardson, J. T. 2023. "Contradictions, Conflicts, Dilemmas and Temporary Resolutions: A Sociology of Law Analysis of Shari'a in Selected Western Societies." In A. Possamai, J. T. Richardson, and B. S. Turner, eds., *The Sociology of Shari'a: Case Studies from around the Globe*, 2nd ed., pp. 303–23. New York: Springer.

Richardson, J. T. 2024. "The Judicialization of Religious Freedom: Comparison of European Court Systems with the United States Supreme Court." In O. Breskaya, R. Finke, and G. Giordan, eds., *Religion between Governance and Freedoms*, 31–46. London: Springer Nature.

Richardson, J. T. Forthcoming, 2025a. "Jehovah's Witnesses and the International Campaign for Religious Freedom." In E. Baran and Z. Knox, eds., *Essays on Minority Religions and Religious Tolerance: The Jehovah's Witness Test*. London: Bloomsbury.

Richardson, J. T. Forthcoming, 2025b. "Judicialization of Politics and Judicialization of Religion in the Two Major Court Systems in Europe." In E. Fokas and A. Giorgi, eds., *Routledge Handbook of Religion and Politics in Europe*. London: Routledge.

Richardson, J. T. and F. Bellanger. 2014. *Legal Cases Involving New Religions and Minority Faiths*. Aldershot: Ashgate.

Richardson, J. T. and C. Borowik. Forthcoming, 2026. "Courts, Children and New Religions: The Impact of a Precedential U.K. Custody Case on The Family (Formerly the Children of God)." In S. Palmer, ed., *Hiding from Herod*. New York: New York University Press.

Richardson, J. T. and R. Davis. 1983. "Experiential Fundamentalism: Revisions of Orthodoxy in the Jesus Movement." *Journal of the American Academy of Religion*, 51, no. 3: 397–425.

Richardson, J. T. and J. DeWitt. 1992. "Christian Science Spiritual Healing, Public Opinion, and the Law." *Journal of Church and State* 34, no. 3: 549–61.

Richardson, J. T. and A. Garay. 2004. "The European Court of Human Rights and Former Communist Countries." In D. Jerolimov, S. Zrinscak, and I. Borowik, eds., *Religion and Patterns of Social Transformation*, 223–34. Zagreb: Institute of Social Research.

Richardson, J. T., M. Harder, and R. Simmonds. 1979. *Organized Miracles: A Study of a Contemporary, Youth, Communal, Fundamentalist Organization*. New Brunswick, NJ: Transaction Books.

Richardson, J. T. and M. Introvigne. 2001. "'Brainwashing' Theories in European Parliamentary and Administrative Reports on 'Cults' and 'Sects.'" *Journal for the Scientific Study of Religion* 40, no. 2: 143–68.

Richardson, J. T. and M. Introvigne. 2007. "New Religious Movements, Countermovements, Moral Panics, and the Media." In D. G. Bromley, ed., *Teaching New Religious Movements*, 91–114. Oxford: Oxford University Press.

Richardson, J. T., G. Krylova, and M. Shterin. 2004. "Legal Regulation in Russia: New Developments." In J. T. Richardson, ed., *Regulating Religion: Case Studies from around the Globe*, 247–57. New York: Kluwer.

Richardson, J. T. and B. Lee. 2014. "The Role of the Courts in the Social Construction of Religious Freedom in Central and Eastern Europe." *Review of Eastern and Central European Law* 39: 291–313.

Richardson, J. T. and B. McGraw. 2019. "Congressional Efforts to Defend and Extend Religious Freedom and the Law of Unintended Consequences." *Religion – Staat – Gesellschaft* 20, no. 1–2: 33–48.

Richardson, J. T. and T. Robbins. 2010. "Monitoring and Surveillance of Religious Groups in the United States." In D. Davis, ed., *The Oxford Handbook of Church and State in the United States*, 354–69. New York: Oxford University Press.

Richardson, J. T., J. Robinson, and D. Schaar-Bias. 2005. "Justice System Degree Programs at the University of Nevada, Reno." *Justice System Journal* 26: 212–18.

Richardson, J. T. and J. Shoemaker. 2007. "The European Court of Human Rights, Minority Religions, and the Social Construction of Religious Freedom," In E. Barker, ed., *The Centrality of Religion in Social Life: Essays in Honour of James A. Beckford*, 103–16. Burlington, VT: Ashgate.

Richardson, J. T. and J. Shoemaker. 2014. "The Resurrection of Religion in the U.S.? The 'Tea' Cases, the Religious Freedom Restoration Act, and the War on Drugs." In J. T. Richardson and F. Bellanger, eds., *Legal Cases, New Religious Movements, and Minority Faiths*, 71–88. London: Ashgate.

Richardson, J. T. and T. C. Sim. 1982. "The IRS and New Religions: A Case Study." Presented at the Annual Meeting of the Society for the Scientific Study of Religion, Providence, RI.

Richardson, J. T. and V. Springer. 2013. "Legal Pluralism and Shari'a in Western Societies: Theories and Hypotheses." In L. Beaman and W. Sullivan, eds., *Varieties of Religious Establishments*, 201–18. London: Ashgate.

Richardson, J. T. and B. S. Turner. 2024. "Shari'a Tribunals in North America." In *Oxford Research Encyclopedia of Religion*. Oxford University Press. https://doi.org/10.1093/acrefore/9780199340378.013.866.

Richardson, J. T. and B. Van Driel. 1994. "New Religions in Europe: A Comparison of Developments and Reactions in England, France, Germany, and The Netherlands." In A. Shupe and D. G. Bromley, eds., *Anti-Cult Movements in Cross-Cultural Perspective*, 129–70. New York: Garland Publishing.

Richardson, J. T., S. Wright, and E. Barker. 2024. "A Quantitative Study of Jehovah's Witnesses in Japan." Paper presented at Annual Meeting of the Scientific Study of Religion, Philadelphia, PA, October.

Rochford, E. B. 1985. *Hare Krishna in America*. New Brunswick, NJ: Rutgers University Press.

Rochford, E. B. 1988. "Movement and Public in Conflict: Values, Finances and the Decline of Hare Krisha." In J. T. Richrdson, ed., *Money and Power in the New Religions*, 271–303. Lweiston, NY: Edwin Mellen Press.

Rochford, E. B. 2007. *Hare Krishna Transformed*. New York: New York University Press.

Rochford, E. B. 2013. "The Changing Faces of God: The Hinduisation of the Hare Krishna." In Eileen Barker, ed., *Revisionism and Diversification in New Religious Movements*, 31–45. Burlington, VT: Ashgate.

Rochford, E. B. 2018. "Aligning Hare Krishna: Political Activists, Hippies, and Hindus." *Nova Religio* 22, no. 1: 34–58.

Rothstein, M. 2004. "Regulating New Religions in Denmark." In J. T. Richardson, ed., *Regulating Religion: Case Studies from around the Globe*, 221–35. New York: Kluwer.

Rothstein, M. 2015. "The Study of New Religions in Denmark: A Brief and Subjective Research History, 1985–2014." In J. Lewis and I. Tollefsen, eds., *Handbook of Nordic Religions*, 15–35. Leiden: Brill.

Roux, E. 2021. "Scientology Behind the Scenes: The Law Changer." In E. Barker and J. T. Richardson, eds., *Reactions to the Law by Minority Religions*, 58–78. London: Routledge.

Sadurski, W. 2009. "Partnering with Strasbourg: Constitutionalization of the European Court of Human Rights." *Human Rights Law Review* 9, no. 3: 397–453.

Scheppele, K. L. 2003. "Constitutional Negotiations: Political Contexts of Judicial Activism in Post-Soviet Europe." *International Sociology* 18: 219–38.

Seiwert, H. 2004. "The German Enquete Commission on Sects: Political Conflicts and Compromises." In J. T. Richardson, ed., *Regulating Religion: Case Studies from around the Globe*, 85–101. New York: Kluwer.

Seiwert, H. 2015. "Religiöser Nonkonformismus in säkularen Gesellschaften." *Zeitschrift für Religionswissenschaft* 23, no. 1: 35–66. https://doi.org/10.1515/zfr-2015-0008.

Shterin, M. 2024. "Russia." *Religious Minorities Online*. De Gruyter. https://doi.org/10.1515/rmo.18838634.

Shterin, M. and J. T. Richardson. 2000. "Effects of the Western Anti-cult Movement on Development of Laws Concerning Religion in Post-communist Russia." *Journal of Church and State* 42, no. 2: 247–72.

Shterin, M. and J. T. Richardson. 2002. "The Yakunin v. Dworkin Case: Analysis of a Major Legal Case Involving Minority Religions in Russia." *Religion in Eastern Europe* 22: 1–38.

Shupe, A. 2009. "The Nature of the New Religious Movements – Anticult 'Culture War' in Microcosm: The Church of Scientology versus the Cult Awareness Network." In J. R. Lewis, ed., *Scientology*, 269–81. Oxford: Oxford University Press.

Shupe, A. and D. G. Bromley. 1980. *The New Vigilantes: Anti-Cultism and the New Religions*. Beverly Hills, CA: Sage.

Shupe, A., R. Spielman, and S. Stigall. 1977. "Deprogramming: The New Exorcism." *American Behavioral Scientist* 20: 941–46.

Singelenberg, R. 2004. "Foredoomed to Failure: The Anti-Cult Movement in the Netherlands." In J. T. Richardson, ed., *Regulating Religion: Case Studies from around the Globe*, 213–19. New York: Kluwer.

Stark, R. and R. Finke. 1992. *The Churching of America, 1776–1990: Winners and Losers in Our Religious Economy*. New Brunswick, NJ: Rutgers University Press.

Stewart, D. and J. T. Richardson. 1999. "Mundane Materialism: How Tax Policies and Other Governmental Regulation Affected Beliefs and Practices of a Jesus Movement Organization." *Journal of the American Academy of Religion* 67, no. 4: 825–47.

Stiansen, O. and E. Voeten. 2019. "Backlash and Judicial Restraint: Evidence from the European Court of Human Rights." SSRN: Retrieved from https://papers.ssrn.com/so13/papers.cfm?abstract_id=3166110.

Stoddard, B. (2024). *The Production of Entheogenic Communities in the United States*. Cambridge: Cambridge University Press.

Strausberg, M., S. Wright, and C. Cusack. 2022. *The Demise of Religion: How Religions End, Die, or Dissipate*. London: Bloomsbury.

Tamanaha, B. 2004. *On the Rule of Law: History, Politics, Theory*. Cambridge: Cambridge University Press.

Tamanaha, B. 2008. "Understanding Legal Pluralism: Past to Present, Local to Global." *Sydney Law Review* 30: 375–411.

Tate, N. and T. Vallinder. 1995. *The Global Expansion of Judicial Power*. New York: New York University Press.

Temperman, J., J. Gunn, and M. Evans. 2019. *The European Court of Human Rights and the Freedom of Religion or Belief: The 25 Years since Kokkinakis*. Leiden: Brill.

Tong, J. 2009. *Revenge of the Forbidden City: Chinese Repression of the Falun Gong*. Oxford: Oxford University Press.

Turner, B. S. and J. T. Richardson. 2024. "Shari'a, Legal Pluralism, and Muslim Arbitration Panel s in the West." In A. Hussain, ed., *Oxford Encyclopedia and Religion*. Oxford: Oxford University Press. https://doi.org/10.1093/acrefore/9780199340378.013.1188.

Urban, H. 2011. *The Church of Scientology*. Princeton, NJ: Princeton University Press.

Urban, H. 2013. "The Church of Scientology." In E. Barker, ed., *Revisionism and Diversification in New Religious Movements*, 65–78. Burlington, VT: Ashgate.

Vasmatics, M. 2021. "Breaking the Twelve-Year European Ban Against Rev. and Mrs. Sun Myung Moon." *The Journal of Unification Studies* 22: 133–52.

Vickers, L. 2021. "Religious Discrimination and Headscarves – Take Two." July 29, https://ohrh.law.ox.ac.uk/religious-discrimination-and-headscarves-take-two/.

Voas, D. 2007. "The Trumpet Sounds Retreat: Learning from the Jehovah's Witnesses." In E. Barker, ed., *The Centrality of Religion in Social Life: Essays in Honour of James A. Beckford*, 117–30. Burlington, VT: Ashgate.

Ward, A. 2009. "Animal Sacrifice." Free Speech Center: Middle Tennessee University: Murfreesboro, Tennessee. Available at: https://firstamendment.mtsu.edu/article/animal-sacrifice/.

Westbrook, D. A. 2018. "The Art of PR War: Scientology, the Media, and Legislative Strategies for the 21st Century." *Studies in Religion* 47: 373–95.

Westbrook, D. A. 2021. "The War Is Not Over: Scientology, Resilience, and the Resurgence of State-Sponsored Anti-Cultism in France." *International Journal for the Study of New Religions* 12: 115–43.

Westbrook, D. A. 2024. *Anticultism in France: Scientology, Religious Freedom, and the Future of New and Minority Religions*. Cambridge: Cambridge University Press.

Wintle, M. 2000. "Pillarisation, Consociation, and Vertical Pluralism in the Netherlands Revisited: A European View." *West European Politics* XXIII, no. 3: 139–152.

Witte, J. and J. Nichols. 2013. "Who Governs the Family? Marriage as a New Test Case of Overlapping Jurisdictions." *Faulkner Law Review* 4: 321–93.

Witte, J. and E. Pin. 2021. "Faith in Strasbourg and Luxembourg? The Fresh Rise of Religious Freedom Litigation in the Pan-European Courts." *Emory Law Journal* 70: 587–661.

Wright, S. A. 1995. *Armageddon in Waco: Critical Perspectives on the Branch Davidian Conflict.* Chicago: University of Chicago Press.

Wright, S. A. and S. J. Palmer, eds. 2016. *Storming Zion: Government Raids on Religious Communities.* Oxford: Oxford University Press.

Wright, S. A. and J. T. Richardson. 2011. *Saints under Siege: The Raid on the Fundamentalist Latter Day Saints in Texas.* New York: New York University Press.

Wright, S. A. and J. T. Richardson. 2014. "The Fundamentalist Latter Day Saints after the Texas State Raid: Assessing the Post-raid Movement Trajectory." *Nova Religio* 17, no. 4: 83–97.

Yang, F. 2006. "The Red, Black, and Gray Markets of Religion in China." *The Sociological Quarterly* 47: 93–122.

Zoehrer, P. 2021. "Legal Challenges Posed to the Unification Church in Europe." In E. Barker and J. T. Richardson, eds., *Reactions to the Law by Minority Religions*, 97–114. London: Routledge.

Zygmunt. 1975. "Jehovah's Witnesses in the U.S.A., 1942–1976." *Social Compass* 24: 45–57.

Cambridge Elements

New Religious Movements

Founding Editor
†James R. Lewis
Wuhan University

The late James R. Lewis was a Professor of Philosophy at Wuhan University, China. He was the author or co-author of 128 articles and reference book entries, and editor or co-editor of 50 books. Most recently was the general editor for the *Alternative Spirituality and Religion Review* and served as the associate editor for the *Journal of Religion and Violence*. His prolific publications include *The Cambridge Companion to Religion and Terrorism* (Cambridge University Press 2017) and *Falun Gong: Spiritual Warfare and Martyrdom* (Cambridge University Press 2018).

Series Editor
Rebecca Moore
San Diego State University

Rebecca Moore is Emerita Professor of Religious Studies at San Diego State University. She has written and edited numerous books and articles on Peoples Temple and the Jonestown tragedy. Publications include *Beyond Brainwashing: Perspectives on Cultic Violence* (Cambridge University Press 2018) and Peoples Temple and Jonestown in the *Twenty-First Century* (Cambridge University Press 2022). She is reviews editor for *Nova Religio*, the quarterly journal on new and emergent religions published by the University of Pennsylvania Press.

About the Series

Elements in New Religious Movements go beyond cult stereotypes and popular prejudices to present new religions and their adherents in a scholarly and engaging manner. Case studies of individual groups, such as Transcendental Meditation and Scientology, provide in-depth consideration of some of the most well known, and controversial, groups. Thematic examinations of women, children, science, technology, and other topics focus on specific issues unique to these groups. Historical analyses locate new religions in specific religious, social, political, and cultural contexts. These examinations demonstrate why some groups exist in tension with the wider society and why others live peaceably in the mainstream. The series highlights the differences, as well as the similarities, within this great variety of religious expressions.

Cambridge Elements

New Religious Movements

Elements in the series

The Sacred Force of Star Wars Jedi
William Sims Bainbridge

Mormonism
Matthew Bowman

Jehovah's Witnesses
Jolene Chu and Ollimatti Peltonen

Wearing Their Faith: New Religious Movements, Dress, and Fashion in America
Lynn S. Neal

Santa Muerte Devotion: Vulnerability, Protection, Intimacy
Wil G. Pansters

J. Krishnamurti: Self-Inquiry, Awakening, and Transformation
Constance A Jones

Making Places Sacred: New Articulations of Place and Power
Matt Tomlinson, Yujie Zhu

Korean New Religions
Don Baker

The Revelation Spiritual Home: The Revival of African Indigenous Spirituality
Massimo Introvigne, Rosita Šorytė

Abuse in New Religious Movements
Sarah Harvey

New Religious Movements and the Romantic Spirit of Modernity
Stef Aupers, Dick Houtman, Galen Watts

Minority Religions, the Law, and the Courts: Cases and Consequences
James T. Richardson

A full series listing is available at: www.cambridge.org/ENRM

For EU product safety concerns, contact us at Calle de José Abascal, 56–1°,
28003 Madrid, Spain or eugpsr@cambridge.org.

www.ingramcontent.com/pod-product-compliance
Lightning Source LLC
LaVergne TN
LVHW011853060526
838200LV00054B/4307